A Handbook for Collaborative Leaders

Millennials Assess the Workplace of today

Rev. Don Broadwell

A HANDBOOK FOR COLLABORATIVE LEADERS
MILLENNIALS ASSESS THE WORKPLACE OF TODAY

iUniverse books may be ordered through booksellers or by contacting:

iUniverse
1663 Liberty Drive
Bloomington, IN 47403
www.iuniverse.com
844-349-9409

Because of the dynamic nature of the Internet, any web addresses or links contained in this book may have changed since publication and may no longer be valid. The views expressed in this work are solely those of the author and do not necessarily reflect the views of the publisher, and the publisher hereby disclaims any responsibility for them.

Any people depicted in stock imagery provided by Getty Images are models, and such images are being used for illustrative purposes only. Certain stock imagery © Getty Images.

ISBN: 978-1-6632-5293-7 (sc)
ISBN: 978-1-6632-5294-4 (e)

Library of Congress Control Number: 2023908265

Print information available on the last page.

iUniverse rev. date: 05/15/2023

Contents

Troubled by his lack of civilian success following an exemplary seven years as a Marine officer, Don Broadwell studied at California's Leader Effectiveness Institute beginning in 1984. On the advice of a career counselor, he began teaching non-hierarchical leadership workshops in order to become the biggest learner in the class. By now, he has thirty years' experience training teachers to collaborate with their students. He captures much of that practice in his books.

Don acts as director-in-training of The Collaborative Center in suburban Maple Valley, Washington (Seattle). Besides his university work, he has performed national workshops for the Association of Federally Employed Women as well as the Association for Experiential Education. He is the author of COLLABORATIVE LEADERSHIP FOR THE CLASSROOM as well as A HANDBOOK FOR COLLABORATIVE LEADERS, Millennials Assess the Workplace of Today. All of Don's work is interactive and revolves around the real-time work experience of his audience.

Preface

Following my time in the Marines and a brief sojourn as a pastor, I worked for forty years among educators. By the fall of 2010, I was pleasantly retired. For keeping busy, for pocket change, and for the company of young people, I delivered pizza on the weekends. One day, on a whim, I googled Collaboration/Obama, and came across a USA Today article, "Obama Bets on Collaboration." That got my attention. I had taught collaborative leadership workshops to teachers for the better part of three decades, withdrawing from that field in 2002 when standardized testing began dominating the school curriculum. Between quarterly workshop teaching at Seattle Pacific University, I had kept my nine-to-five job supplying picture books and readers to northwest school libraries. This placed me in the position of absorbing the ever-present critique of education while having the trust of librarians, who often shared with me their dismay. As a book rep, I have been education's proverbial fly in the wall, listening and watching as everyone from the Koch brothers to the Gates Foundation, to the U.S. Congress seemed to know more about teaching than the professionals who performed it. I had been intrigued when, in the 1990s, under the rubric of *"decentralized decision-making,"* collaboration was tried and found wanting. Could a return to collaborative deciding be at hand?

My interest grew the further I searched. At length, I discovered President Obama's initiative on collaboration, the Open Innovation Portal, and its one half-billion program for promising new ideas.

After years of lobbying for children's voices in classroom decision-making, I found the invitation I had sought. After a decade-long thrust toward standardized testing, the teacher/student relationship, once fostered by preeminent educator John Dewey, would finally come back to the spotlight. . .. or so I thought.

At the building level, indicating deliberations between administrators and staff during the Human Potential days of the 1990s, participative leading was the rage. But participation proved to be clumsy, time-consuming, and unproductive. By the year 2,000, top-down leading returned in force. Command and control once more became the accepted modality, certainly in practice. *"It's always been this way; it's always going to be this way; and there's nothing you can do about it."* Participative decision-making continued to get lip service. But given the time needed for group deliberations and the confusion over method – not to mention the lack of accountability – the collapse of "participation" should have been foreseen. Surely by 2010, the time had come for me to dip my toe back in the water. I re-booted my Collaborative Center, reconnected with Seattle Pacific University, and found myself on campus once again.

In general, leadership has undergone many changes since the early days of civilization. Indeed, the Industrial Revolution called for a rational, model, and this was provided by Frederick Taylor's Principles of Scientific Management, first published in 1911. Taylor, however, overlooked much that the ancients had to offer. Some 500 years before Christ, Lao Tzu is recorded saying, "A leader is best when people barely know he exists." We know much about what a leader is. He is tall, male, well groomed; he is industrious, ambitious, and visionary. He is confident, deliberate in actions, and circumspect in thought.

But what does the leader *do* exactly? Leaders solve problems. They do more than drive people with alpha male demands (the transactional model), more than inviting workers to share in the mission and goals (the transformational model). Leaders do more than meet employee's needs (Greenleaf's servant model). Despite being conceived by Dr. Thomas Gordon in the early 1960s, the collaborative model of problem-solving, where the needs of both management and employee are recognized, then balanced, remains new and innovative. Time will tell if there is room for Gordon's model among our nation's workforce, or as I argue in chapter 4, there is merit to a flexible mix of styles, one that proves facile, productive, spontaneous, and even beguiling for employee and employer alike.

My first exposure to leadership came some 60 years ago at the benevolent auspices of the U.S. Marine Corps. Following three months of Officer Candidate School and six months command training, I got my first assignment to lead an infantry platoon at Camp Pendleton, California. Following eighteen months of infantry duty, I was moved to the USMC Mountain Warfare Training Center in California's High Sierras. There, along with twelve other guides, I was tasked to train marines in the science of over-snow combat and, during the summer, in the practice of cliff assault. The Marines we trained each month would not form a fighting unit in and of themselves. They were expected to serve as advisor/guides to large-scale operations should warfare break out at high elevations, which it has . . . just not in 1962.

After 30 months in the mountains, I bounced between desk jobs, then took my leave to study pastoral counseling. My seminary training gave me my first exposure to group decision-making, and though I didn't fully understand it, I have never looked back. I have watched as group-process leading (as it was called in the 1960s) morphed into conflict resolution, then into conflict prevention, negotiated leadership, no-lose leading, participatory leading, and now leading via collaboration. Collaboration is a suitable description. It is at the very center of innovation in the tech industry. Today, considering the many exhortations to collaborate, all that is missing is how, and when, topics I address in this book. "The issues and problems are so complex that no one person can supply the necessary leadership to get results" (Chrislip & Larson, p. 143).

Former NYPD commissioner Bill Bratton's book Collaborate or Perish! cites leaders of commerce and civics working together to solve mutual problems at the highest level of organization (Bratton and Tumin, 2012, p. 8). Still Bratton does not address those thorny day-to-day problems that stifle creativity, degrade production, and damage morale. What about the employee who is always late? How about a dispute on the factory floor? What to do with the worker who insists the boss is wrong? Or who fights off direction? These instances make up the thrust of my book. Today, considering the many exhortations to collaborate, all that is missing is when and how. These are the topics I address in this book. Among the chapters on collaboration is a unique take on the Situational Leadership of Hersey/Blanchard. In chapter 4, I argue that supervisors are better served to include influences outside the group as well as those within. This is the section that reconciles Authority with Participatory leading.

I am indebted to Captain (later Major General) Ort Steele for showing me the human side of authority while we were assigned to the Mountain Warfare Center in California's High Sierras. Among other things, Steele told me to quit insisting the marines salute me. "You never know when you'll need these guys to dig you out from a pile of snow." I took his advice. His was the first of many burning bush moments for me. I remember the times that followed as the closest of team bonding. They were among the happiest and most challenging of my career.

The day Steele joined us at the Mountain Leadership School, he invited me for a run. As we jogged in the crisp mountain air, he plied me with questions about his new job. Who were the guides he would be working with? What should he expect from us? What did we expect from him? He was quick to assure me I would have a job as his assistant, and soon placed me in charge of the winter syllabus. Since he was a novice skier, he quickly became my pupil. I was beneath him in rank, and I revered him for naming me his second during the winter phase of training. (Another lieutenant got the well-deserved second-in-command during our climbing syllabus.) My esteem for Ort Steele has never waned.

From Captain Steele, I learned never to issue an order I could not expect to enforce. Also, nobody knows how to do the job better than the man who is doing it. Don't tell people how to do things, instead tell when what you want done and leave them alone. This advice actually goes to Gen. George Patton, who said, "Never tell people how to do things. Tell them what to do and they will surprise you with their ingenuity." Unlike Patton, who had a gruff reputation, Steele carried a gentility that would make Gone with the Wind's Rhett Butler proud; during our years together, I never heard him raise his voice. He was an ideal example of classic command-and-control, where the leader solves problems, makes decisions and issues orders, but not without consulting subordinates.

I will try to emulate Ort Steele as I write. I will not raise my voice. There is nothing in this book that one ought to do to become an effective leader. There are no shoulds, no oughts, no musts. There is only invitation. You will discover you are already more of a leader than you realize. "The fact is, however, there is nothing inherently unpleasant about collaboration. Working together to solve a problem, envision a future, or make a decision, can be an enjoyable and even energizing experience" (Straus, 2002, p. 3)

Introduction

Something happened to The Hierarchy on the way to the 21st Century. For generations, this beacon on the horizon was the industrial table of organization and with it, that pyramid of power which determined who could give direction to whom. The Hierarchy also brought accountability, stability, and order to an unwieldly industrial behemoth. Its most influential advocate, Frederick Taylor, whose Scientific Steps of Management (1911) governed leader behavior for the better part of one hundred years, was a slave to it. Although modified in modern times (see Tom Gordon, chapter 2), Taylor's scientific steps burdened leaders with an all-wise level of authority, and it is not accepted by workers today. Why not? Those millennials! Minted during the 1980s, by the year 2,000, Millennials began exercising their workplace 'rights' according to the way they had been schooled. Self-esteem and assertiveness now propel them to share their every idea, as though Facebook were the business platform of the moment. This spells more than background noise; it means Millennials are itching for a piece of the action, whether employers like it or not. More than one boss has complained, "I tell them what to do and they just don't get it done" (Kelly, B., personal exchange, 2020). Of course! It simply was not their idea. Ownership, even authorship were missing. Can we somehow expand the voices of Millennials to where they help determine outcomes in the cubicles? The factory floor? The agency offices? What model will leaders adhere to? And what does collaboration have to do with leadership?

It must have some bearing, for as Professor William Glasser once wrote, "Boss management fails because it limits both the quality of the work and the production of the worker. Its use actually causes most of the problems we are trying to prevent" (Glasser, 1998). Harvard's Rosabeth Moss-Kanter was more prophetic, "The hierarchy is dead. It just hasn't fallen yet" (Moss-Kanter, 1989). My goal is for employers, supervisors, and other leaders to share their decision-making with workers, to model collaborative leading in situations of choice.

A Handbook for Collaborative Leaders follows a developmental format, meaning I use a building block scheme to add small units to those already learned. Chapter 1 describes the evolution of leadership thought from Lao Tzu, writing prior to the Christian Era, through the 1990s Human Potential Movement to the Obama-inspired emphasis on collaboration. Chapter 2 describes collaboration under basic conditions—for example, when there is no upset and no hidden agenda. Here, full disclosure is in place. It is the best way I know to teach collaboration's fundamentals. Chapter 3 details how to collaborate amid complications like angry feelings and when stakeholders are not forthcoming. This chapter includes when there are multiple stakeholders and when there is no third-party facilitator to help.

In chapter 4, I examine twin-poled leading, flexible problem-solving that originates along a spectrum. Here I create a new understanding of Situational Leadership, a succeeding synthesis on the conventional Hersey/Blanchard design. Here the key ingredient is personal values. The role played by values is spelled out so there is no doubt that authority and collaboration are both valid starting places for leaders; the two exist side-by-side, or rather end to end along a bi-polar spectrum. (We train young baseball players to keep their eyes on the ball – the only way to assure that their hands will maneuver to contact the target. The same applies to personal values. When leadership values are known, spelled out and placed front and center, collaboration becomes one of many problem-solving choices, but it can be the option of first refusal, as leaders shift their base away from long-established authority).

Chapter 5 elaborates on my twin-poled, or bi-polar model. It shows how leading divides into a two-step sequence -- deciding how to decide and then, deciding. Leaders can subsequently 'base' their decisions in a preferred position on the chart. Chapter 6 studies the education of today's workers and looks at generational changes that point to collaboration as an optimal style. Case study examples punctuate the prose. These stem from my experience as a trainer and revolve around material from the world of education as well as the workplace.

Chapter 7 explores today's partisan drama unleashed by the Democratic vote. Onetime DC school superintendent and political diva Michelle Rhee once argued, "The civil rights movement didn't work things out by consensus" (Rhee 2010, para 9.), but for workplace, community, and political reform in the twenty first century, collaboration is a choice for *reaching* consensus. Civic leaders will find it easier to shape their constituents into a problem-solving whole than to be the all-knowing decider. They can energize their constituents, gain buy-in, and implement solutions together with their charges. Leading becomes as stress free an activity as reading a book or eating lunch. In the process, leaders can raise cooperation to levels they covet and desire.

Whether within government or inside the corporate community, collaborative leadership brings challenges. Before long Generation Z will join Millennials demanding inclusion in the discourse. Leaders who collaborate will more easily adjust their expectations to this multi-generational workforce. At first, employees will not understand that collaboration is for special occasions. It is not meant to take over decision-making. Also, senior officials need to understand the collaborative process in order to evaluate their staff. To those who say collaboration takes too much time, I argue implementing work plans is a clear and present advantage. *Employees will do what they decide to do*, and that includes when they help forge the final solution. "Harnessing the power of collaborative action requires a different model of leadership than the classic 'command-and-control' in which the leader solves problems, makes decisions, and issues directives unilaterally. Indeed, the old model is antithetical to building a creative corporate culture." (Straus, 2002, p. 146). Building this culture is the goal of this book.

Once the culture is under way, managers who collaborate release the creative energy of their charges, facilitate the resulting discussion, gain buy-in from stakeholders, and find implementing outcomes easier thanks to the engagement of their people. Millennials, despite their opinionated attitudes are ideally suited to a bi-polar culture where leaders no longer solve problems, instead *they see that problems get resolved*. Like Tom Gordon, I believe the terms leadership and problem-solving are interchangeable. Here, as in Leader Effectiveness Training (Gordon, 1957, p. 27), the terms are synonymous. This assertion has proven itself time and again over my thirty years of teaching. Still, the evidence is anecdotal and the time left waiting for empirical proof is short. (See epilogue)

Chapter 1

A Brief History of Leadership

"We now know that along with everything else, leadership changes"
Barbara Kellerman

I remember the moment when for me, leadership changed forever. As freshly minted pastor of a small New Jersey church, I was tasked with organizing our high school fellowship for a Christmas pageant. Although steeped in authority-based deciding, during the months prior to the event, I had taken loose rein with my kids, placing myself as a listener more than a director. But I had longed for a more hands-on role. The notion of thirty plus youngsters needing what I thought was a Hollywood-style director was the perfect chance for me to take charge. With no hesitation, I waded in, giving orders left and right. My kids were confused and upset. My misadventure ended when the group's president came to me with, "We want you out of here." Another epiphany! Twelve years later I would learn ways I could have stayed in character and still met the group's need for direction. For the moment, I was stunned. I was not over it when a few youngsters came over to see if I was okay. Since that day I have learned more lessons, *some of which I liked.*

This I learned above all else; leadership has always changed. It does so today in the cubicles, in the classroom, in the boardroom and on the factory floor. Methods once embraced are now shunned. As new methods emerge, managers give them a try to see if they are effective. In the pages to come, we'll examine how leadership in general has changed through the ages. Such a historical perspective can help you understand why and how your leadership will change over time. A big-picture view is important. So, let's dive right in!

NOTE: The material to come is meant as an overview to put the methodologies in a larger context. Readers may wish to skip to chapter two, collaboration's fundamentals.

From its inception in the pre-Christian era to the mid-20th century, leadership's change rate has been slow. Over the past 70 years that pace increased to something surprisingly intense. Today leadership is in a quandary. Training is a fifty billion dollar per year industry despite bringing us no closer to nirvana than we were previously. "Bottom line; while the leadership industry has been thriving – growing and prospering beyond anyone's early imaginings – leaders by and large are performing poorly, worse in many ways than before" (Kellerman, 2012, p. xv). How to account for this apparent disconnect when, in fact leadership and followership have both evolved over time? Let us start from the beginning.

From the start of recorded history, kings, princes, and clerics ruled the masses -- so much so that by the 17 century, philosopher Thomas Hobbes framed life as "solitary, brutish, poor, nasty, and short" (Leviathan, I. xiii). Still there had evolved leaders concerned with whom to lead and how. In the beginning, there were Lao Tzu, Confucius, Socrates, and Plato. Confucius (551 B.C.) believed that those in authority should behave as gentlemen. Self-educated, and without an official platform from which to teach, he organized groups of disciples and taught them the elements of leadership he embraced.

Confucius was disturbed by the authoritarian condition of his time, dedicating his life to social reform. His Analects (teachings), compiled by students after his death, revealed his primary emphasis on sincerity and his commitment to ethical leadership. He advocated that leaders should be older, wiser, better, as close to perfection as possible. He taught, "Those who wished to secure the good of others should have already secured their own" (Anderson, 1990, p. 52). Confucius believed that government should make as its end the happiness of its subjects, not the pleasure of the rulers. Confucius has been called perhaps the most influential teacher in the history of the world (Anderson, 1990, p. 50).

Plato (423 B.C.) was a contemporary of Confucius in focus and in thought, if a century younger by birth. He too believed in the education of leaders and surrounded himself with students at the Academy of Athens, which he founded. He believed that leading was based in wisdom, and that unless philosophers become kings, or kings become philosophers, cities will have no rest from troubles nor, he surmised, will the human race (Plato p.473). "Confucius's gentleman leader and Plato's philosopher-king have elements in common. They aspire to perfection, reflect a context that is leader-centric, and they are of a historical moment in which good governance seemed completely to depend on good, even great leadership" (Carlyle, 1841). The notion of the valiant leader did not begin to wane until 1215, when King John of England was compelled to sign the Magna Carta, admitting that his authority was not absolute, and his will could not be arbitrarily put to work. This should have been a benchmark in the history of leadership, but the Great Man theory would not fade easily. It would take another 750 years before scholarship would join reality in promoting gender-neutral leadership and exploring the prospect of leader and follower laboring together to decide.

Change, in other words, was glacial. Although the Magna Carta was a watershed in which the king was compelled to succumb to his followers, this was, after all, the Middle Ages, when royalty ruled on earth and when God, through the Catholic Church, ruled the masses.

It is extraordinary then, that the most durable, the most secular, the most pragmatic of leadership treatises was Niccolo Machiavelli's The Prince (1513). Without at least a casual reading of Machiavelli, one easily falls into the commonplace misunderstanding, using the pejorative term 'Machiavellian' to indicate cruelty as a sought-after leader trait.

In fact, Machiavelli was primarily intent on preservation – of his principality, of peace in the domain, and certainly of his power. "As such, he is grounded in the here and now, does not bow to a moral compass, either religious or otherwise, and his loyalty is to himself and his subjects only" (Kellerman, 2012, p. 9). Machiavelli believed his stopovers into cruelty were necessary based on his diminished faith in the human condition. Followers, to Machiavelli, were "fickle, ungrateful, pretenders and dissemblers, evaders of danger, eager for gain" (Machiavelli, 1513). This, together with a glut of crises in the Medici reign, made cruelty a viable option. Consequently, the leader should be good, but *able to be not good*. In any event, Machiavelli viewed cruelty as less abhorrent than a leader's mercy, since "too much mercy allows disorders to continue from which come killings or robberies, activities that hurt the whole community" (The Prince, 1532, p. 65).

Like Machiavelli, Thomas Hobbes, whose Leviathan followed The Prince by 120 years, was concerned with keeping order in a disorderly world. Like Machiavelli, Hobbes thought followers untrustworthy; they were fearful, rapacious, selfish, and dangerous. He too, argued for an authoritarian, even a totalitarian ruler (the Leviathan of his title). Yet unlike Machiavelli, Hobbes turned his attention from those with power to those without. His focus became followers' rights, specifically to a quality life (Hobbes 1651, Chapt. vi). For Hobbes, life under medieval rule was, as mentioned, solitary, poor, nasty, brutish and short.* The sea change he promoted would make at least one right of ordinary people superior to any right of

---

* The life expectancy for males during Hobbes's era was 43.6 years. (Woodbury, 2014, para. 3)

their king, the right to life. "The change from an orientation by natural duties to an orientation by natural rights finds its most potent expression in the ideas of Hobbes, who put the unconditional right to life at the center of his argument" (Kellerman, 2012, p. 9). For Hobbes, this quid-pro-quo was simple and revealing – followers would grant absolute power to a ruler who would in turn, protect them, first to secure their right to life and second, to provide them with a life well lived. This was Hobbes' social contract, a first.

Hobbes and Machiavelli seem of a piece. However, Hobbes based his need for an authoritarian ruler on a different premise, his trade-off of power for protection. John Locke (1632), would expand the rights of ordinary people to include the right to liberty and to own property. This was again, a social contract in which government claims derive their legitimacy from the consent of the governed. Locke insisted that unless the leader satisfies the led, he may be recalled, if necessary, by force (Locke, 1689).

Leadership from the Eighteenth to Mid-20th Century

The period leading up to the American Revolution focused on leadership as a function of authority. Following either Hobbes or Locke, one is led to the need for Authority, whether for authority's sake or for the masses. There followed a period during which that focus remained intact. The question for leaders became, what makes the leader great? For Tolstoy, given his extraordinary faith in the Divine, the answer was that history is predetermined. As such, kings are slaves to history. For Carlyle (1841), history is tantamount to the history of great men who lived and worked here. Moreover, considering the writings of philosophers Herbert Spencer and William James, none of their work dealt directly with leading. It simply tried to answer one of the knottiest questions of the time: Does the man make history, or does history make the man? It fell to philosopher John Stuart Mill (1859) to redirect scholarship to the relationship between leader and follower. This he did by expanding the limit of power to be suffered by the community, a limitation he called the very meaning of liberty.

Not unlike companion philosophers, Mill agreed that "to prevent weaker members of a community from being preyed on by innumerable vultures, it was needful that there should be an animal of prey stronger than the rest, commissioned to keep them down" (Mill, 1859). But as the alpha vulture might also prey on the masses, it was necessary to defend against his intrigues. Therefore, the aim of patriots was to limit the king's power.

Mill was not merely preaching against abuse of the magistrate's strength, but also against the pressure of social convention (what today we would call PC, politically correct). He believed there needs to be protection from the tyranny of public opinion, possibly because he kept a lover for thirty years, marrying her only after her husband died. The romantic collaboration between Harriet Taylor and John Stuart Mill provided Mill with the inspiration to pen one of his greatest essays on liberty, The Subjugation of Women, called "an ardent argument for equality between the sexes, and a consequence of her influence" (Kellerman, 2010, p. 73).

Beyond freedom from harm at the magistrates' hands, Mill believed man should be free to form his own opinions, then to act on them without hindrance so long as the risk and peril are his own. "Neither one person, nor any number of persons, is warranted in saying to another human of ripe years, that he shall not do with his life for his own benefit what he chooses to do with it. He is the person most interested in his own well-being: the interest which any other person, except in cases of strong personal attachment, can have in it, is trifling compared with that which he himself has. The most ordinary man or woman has means of knowledge immeasurably surpassing those that can be possessed by anyone else" (Mill, 1859). [Compare Oliver Wendell Holmes's, "My freedom to swing my arm ends with the other man's nose."]

Mill's writing echoes through our Declaration of Independence and even the songs of Jimi Hendrix. "You have to forget about what other people say, when you're supposed to die, or when you're supposed to be loving. You have to forget about these things."* Although he ignored the darker side of the human condition, Mill is on record as "the most vigorous and optimistic defender of the better angels of our nature" (Kellerman, 2010, p. 73).

Following the Middle Ages Karl Marx and Friedrich Engels (1848), concerned themselves with those without power, authority, or influence. The two were concerned with the role of followership, particularly in inciting revolution. They are in the tradition of literature as leadership, rather than being actual leaders. Marx was a sociologist, educated in philosophy and law; Engels was a merchant committed to overthrowing the German monarchy. The historical leader, the man who followed the blueprint of Engels and Marx, was Russia's Vladimir Lenin.

One contemporary of Lenin was the mechanical engineer, Frederick Taylor. Taylor believed that workers were motivated by money. He contrived the idea that piecework and strict supervision would raise performance levels during the heyday of the Industrial Revolution. As such, he invented tools to streamline workers at U.S. Steel, calculating their every move through the use of a stopwatch. By the 1930s, Taylor's reliance on time-and-motion studies fell out of favor (and were outlawed by congress), but his Scientific Steps of Management was a breakthrough, lending form and substance to what leaders actually do – solve problems. Taylor's scientific steps -- Identify the problem, create alternate solutions, choose one, and implement – would resurface in the work of Thomas Gordon some fifty years later, but not without changes.

Taylor was a rough-and-tumble authoritarian, sharing his dim view of human nature with Hobbes, Machiavelli and the many who came before him. That view was about to shift, with consequences for leaders everywhere.

---

* Compare, Life, Liberty, and the Pursuit of Happiness in our Declaration of Independence.

Rev. Don Broadwell

Postwar Changes in the Psychology of Leading

Next in the pedigree of leadership is Abraham Maslow. The entire thrust of post-World War II leadership pivots around Maslow's *prewar* study which led to his Hierarchy of Human Needs. Maslow's needs hierarchy is well established in psychological literature and to a sizable extent in management. What is less known is Maslow lived and studied among the Lakota Sioux during one summer of the 1930s to learn how Native Americans grew into adulthood. From this Maslow formulated stages of development that are pursued by individuals, and, as we will see, even civilizations. He published his hierarchy in 1954, in time to profoundly influence the leadership theorists (Thomas Gordon in particular) for the ensuing seventy plus years.

Maslow criticized traditional psychology for its study of the sick (Sigmund Freud) and/or animals (B.F. Skinner). He held that a study of normal people would create more and better health among individuals and society-at-large. His axiom -- that people had a strong desire to fulfill their potential -- stands as a paradigm shift in the way we look at men and women in the workplace. His is the seminal development in the study of leadership that influenced scholarship (and management) up to and including the present.

Maslow's hierarchy of needs (see below) states that humans are motivated by the pursuit of unmet needs. According to this theory, if fundamental needs are not satisfied, then one will be compelled to satisfy them. Higher needs such as social and esteem needs are not recognized until one satisfies needs basic to existence (air, water, food, safety). While such pursuit is not linear – individuals move up and down the needs hierarchy and even reach multiple successes at the same time – Maslow's model can nevertheless be used to chart advancement in social cultures as well as in mapping individual fulfillment.

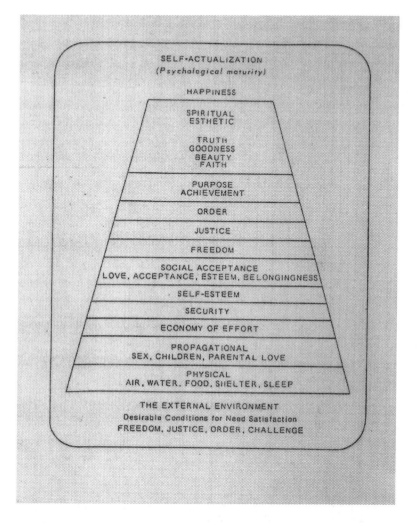

My intent here is not to analyze Maslow's pioneering work so much as it is to pinpoint its seldom noted uniqueness. For the most part, Western circles -- North American culture in particular -- have satisfied basic human needs. What intrigues us is Maslow's Meta, or *growth* needs, in which social and esteem needs become the primary goal. Note how our schools have prepared young people to achieve their social and esteem needs. Meta needs, meaning friendship, belonging to a group, giving and receiving love, and eventually recognition, attention, social status, accomplishment, and self-respect, are the preeminent needs of our present society. Those are especially keen among Millennials. Thanks to the courage and stamina of teachers, those needs are honored in the classroom, even if misunderstood by education's critics, notably advocates of Frederick Taylor and his Scientific Steps.

An early disciple of Maslow, and the man who gets credit for spoiling the Hobbesian view of human nature, was Douglas MacGregor. MacGregor was in fact, a contemporary of Maslow who conceived the notion that people were not averse to work (the old Theory X),˙ rather that work can be as natural as play if the conditions are favorable (MacGregor's Theory Y). In The Human Side of Enterprise (1960), MacGregor noted people will be self-directed to meet work objectives, will be committed to quality and productivity, but only if rewards are in place that address higher needs. Moreover, most people can handle responsibility because creativity and ingenuity are common in the working population. MacGregor makes the point that a command-and-control environment is not effective because it relies on lower needs for motivation.

In Western society, lower needs are substantially met. Thus, they no longer motivate. In a Top-Down environment, one would expect employees to dislike their work, to avoid responsibility, to have no interest in organizational goals, to resist change, etc., thus creating a self-fulfilling prophecy for their leaders. To MacGregor, "motivation seems more likely with Theory Y" (MacGregor, 2015, pg. 4).

Next in line are the men who leveraged Maslow's Hierarchy to create leader models of their own -- Thomas Gordon, Roger Fisher, and William Ury. As we will see in the next chapter (Basic Collaboration), Gordon redefined interpersonal problems so that they reflect the underlying needs of contrasting positions. For example, in an employee--employer disagreement, the parties might

---

˙ Theory X; Most people find work innately distasteful, and they will attempt to avoid it.

join forces in search of fresh solutions, then decide which is best for meeting the needs of both. Gordon's book, Leader Effectiveness Training (1957) sold millions and was a regular on best-seller lists for more than two years. More about Tom Gordon in chapter four.

Fisher and Ury (Getting to Yes; Negotiating Agreement Without Giving In, 1981), cofounders of the Harvard Negotiation Project, differ from Tom Gordon's work in that they prefer the term 'underlying interests' to Gordon's underlying needs -- understandable since their project is aimed at Corporate America. Where Gordon's efforts targeted interpersonal problems that stifle teamwork and creativity, Fisher and Ury's canvas is the corridors of power. For example, during the 1980s, negotiations between the Simpson Lumber Company and the federal government revealed the following interests. Faced with the Spotted Owl controversy, Simpson needed a promise of long-range sustainability and the feds needed protection for the endangered species. Together the sides produced the well-known solution that created islands of tree stands, a home for the endangered birds. "In this different kind of leadership, leaders promote and safeguard the collaborative process rather than take unilateral, decisive action. The power of position is of little help in this world of peers" (Chrislip & Larson, 1994, p. 127). The government found the collaborative process so inviting, it offered Simpson a ten-year moratorium on federal oversight of the company's forests.

In another example, Alaskan fishermen for decades had been herded by the Federal Fisheries Department into fishing on designated days, like hunters who find their prey in season. Halibut fishermen were intensely troubled because when "season" arrived, they were forced to ply their waters without benefit of reliable weather. On average, five men/women were killed each year "Derby Day" was in effect. Collaborating with their Halibut men, Alaska fishing authorities solved the problem by limiting the season to a given number of days yet allowing boats to go out at the discretion of the crew. Today the total purse is shared by the boats on a pro-rated basis. The new schedule protected the Halibut species while preserving human life. The resulting regulation created high morale among the fleet and made millionaires out of many of its crew.

Together with Tom Gordon, Fisher and Ury are responsible for much that transpired in leadership circles during the 1990s. During that decade, the transactional leadership of Machiavelli, Hobbes, and others was replaced by transformational leadership, designed to unite leader and follower using group decision making. For the transactional leader, decisions are pronounced. [One leader who personified transactional leadership was President Harry ("The buck stops here") Truman. Another would be George ("I am the decider") Bush.] Contrariwise, transformational leaders 'sell' their vision to employees, stimulating a shared mission among their team. Where the transactional leader believes optimal solutions stem from contrasting (read conflicting) positions, the transformational leader believes peak solutions originate through commitment to a vision, or idea. One form of transformational leadership is the workforce mission statement, a product of decentralized deciding in the 1990s.

Next in leadership's lineage is the Servant Leadership of Robert Greenleaf. Writing as a contemporary of Thomas Gordon, Greenleaf opined "Servant-leaders focus primarily on the growth and well-being of people and the communities to which they belong. While outmoded leadership involves the accumulation and exercise of power by one at the top of the hierarchy, servant leadership upends the pyramid. The servant-leader yields power, puts the needs of others first and helps people perform as highly as possible" (Greenleaf, 1970, p.5). Well known leadership theorists such as Ken Blanchard, Stephen Covey, and Margaret Wheatley are among those who subscribe to servant leadership.

Greenleaf turns the traditional leadership hierarchy on its head, idealistic on its own and a hard concept to visualize in practice. Nevertheless, in short form, we can say the transactional leader controls power, the transformational leader shares power and the servant leader shuns power altogether. Greenleaf assumes employees whose needs are addressed will labor graciously for their employer's needs at the same time. Unlike Greenleaf, Gordon's method called for unmet needs to be aired and addressed by employer and employee collectively. Gordon called his design method three – method one was where the employer decided. Method two was when employees usurped the decision making. (When describing his method, Gordon additionally referred to 'no-lose' leadership). Needs can be balanced and satisfied through the collaborative process, mentioned above. So, why don't we collaborate? Gordon explained that leaders of the future will have the skills of a counselor. Using these skills is an art, really, based not on content but on a discrete, proven, process. Most people are uninformed about a process that they have never been taught. Collaborative leading is where we turn next, beginning with the basics.

Chapter 2

Basic Collaboration

*"Where in the world is someone who can
teach children how to collaborate?*
Hank Rubin, Collaborative Leadership

Remember the Age of Empowerment? Of decentralized decision-making? Of the flattened hierarchy? The 1990s were billed as the time when workers were granted access to decision-making. By the turn of the century, group meetings, many poorly timed and crudely organized, faced a backlash that resulted in the dismantling of shared decision making and the restoring of Command-and-Control. As the noteworthy Kappan Magazine observed in 2010, "Teacher collaboration is a prime determinant of school improvement. Unfortunately, though we talk about it a lot, we don't do it as much as we might hope for. We take pride when we see a few random acts of collaboration in our schools, but the *modal* behavior in schools has changed little over the years." (Piercey, 2010, p. 55).

As readers might imagine, participatory leading in the 21st century, unlike the amorphous meetings of the 1990s, will operate from a structured, well-defined framework. Similarly, collaborating will mean more than partnering. Anyone can lead a collaborative, but to lead *collaboratively?* That is a different animal indeed.

Collaborative leadership, as envisioned by Dr. Thomas Gordon during the second half of the twentieth century, designates a problem-solving sequence. By the Gordon method, it means a six-step arc that closely resembles Taylor's Scientific Steps. But, by focusing on human needs, Gordon removes power from the leader and involves followers *equally with superiors* when deciding. Gordon redefines problems in such a way that underlying interests are acknowledged, and in fact, achieved. It is truly a 'no-lose' proposition, and that is one moniker it gained when Gordon promoted it in 1957, (also the *No-Lose* method of leadership (Gordon, 1957, p. 217). Dr. Gordon and the man who mentored him are where we turn next.

A Legacy of Mentors

Gordon earned his Ph.D. in psychology in the 1950s having been enamored with the work of Abraham Maslow and with Maslow's Hierarchy of Human Needs. It occurred to Gordon that worker needs were often obscured by managers' focus on productivity, on control. Still such needs appeared valid and if expressed openly, might be accepted by the supervisor. The trick would be to get manager and employee to reveal their needs, and here the gentle prodding of the psychologist in Gordon shone through.

At the University of Chicago, Gordon wrote his dissertation on including followers when making decisions, calling it Group Centered Leadership. His work was roundly dismissed. Not to be disabused of his idea, Gordon published his dissertation, Leader Effectiveness Training, independently. It became an instant hit and remained on the New York Times Best Seller list for more than two years. The book, in its 35th edition can be obtained at Amazon, Barnes and Noble, and through Gordon's legacy institute in Solana Beach, California.

I met Dr. Gordon through my reading and through his Leader Effectiveness Institute in Solana Beach, now Gordon Training International, where I studied in 1984. For his efforts at re-defining workplace problem-solving, Gordon received three nominations for the Nobel Peace Prize. His dream of obtaining a Nobel was never granted and he passed away in 2002.

The Gordon Innovation

Gordon believed the *presenting* problem – the adversarial event as viewed by opposing parties – was seldom the dilemma. He also believed that conflicting ideas no longer promise the path to the best solution. The real problem lay hidden among human needs. For leaders, the challenge is to identify those needs and set them in balance. Gordon wrote that leaders would be more effective if they asked, "*How can we meet the needs of employee A at the same time we meet the needs of employer B?*" (Writing in 1957, Gordon argued that future leaders would have the skills of a counselor.)

In a simple, even elegant example, teacher Leanne Aten was having trouble keeping the halls quiet when her fifth graders returned from recess. When she collaborated with her class, she learned that her students needed a few minutes to unwind. Leanne's need was not to disturb the other classrooms, and when she asked, "How can we have both?" her problem disappeared in a slew of ideas from her kids. "Now I allow them a little time to visit when returning to the room. My students are quiet in the halls, and they have a few minutes to chat. The conflict no longer exists!"

This is the Gordon method at work. But because it involves a concrete sequence and not merely a single innovation, it invites a closer look.

The Set-Up

There are two moments when collaborations come to grief. They are included among Gordon's steps. One he called the Set-Up and the other the Cross-Check. The set-up is where the leader gains permission to influence a new process. This set-up is meant to shut the door on rivals who might bow out before the collaboration is complete. The cross-check helps parties understand one another at a new level, that of human needs. It also promotes commitment to the process once under way. More will be said about the cross-check as we move through collaborative examples in the text.

Here is Leanne, setting the stage;

"I explained to my class that we have a problem and that I would like to solve it in a way that we would all feel good. I asked the class if this was a good time, and if anyone felt it was not enough time we could reschedule. No one raised their hand. I explained that I had taken a class designed to help solve situations where both sides are happy with the outcome. I asked permission to use this strategy, and everybody agreed."

The importance of the set-up cannot be overstated. Without it, the path is open to anyone who wants to defect or wants to sabotage because of some unstated need. The preamble goes like this:

- Introduce oneself as a facilitator rather than a decider.
- State the purpose (so both sides win).
- Ask if the time is good.
- Ask if it is enough time.
- Ask if workers are willing to try something new.
- Begin by directly assessing needs.

Again, do not underestimate the importance of each item in this sequence. Leaders might not have control of the outcome; they trade that for control of the *process*. Such firm control is asserted right from the start. Employers should feel collaboration's reins within their grasp.

Gordon's Six-Step Model

Once the set-up is complete, parties are ready for the Gordon steps. That process shows below so the reader can view the roadmap, the concept in total. We will dive deeply into each step to see how it works, and how you can apply it to your own leadership overview. The steps in order are, (following the Set-Up).

1. Define the problem in terms of the needs of both sides. (Perform the Cross-Check to complete the problem definition).
2. Brainstorm for solutions.
3. Evaluate those ideas.
4. Choose the most acceptable solution.
5. Implement it.
6. Follow up on progress.

These steps, including the crosscheck between steps one and two, are next explained in detail. (The following section assumes collaboration is best learned from the position of third-party facilitator. In the above example, Leanne acted as both stakeholder and facilitator, normally a dicey way to learn.)

Step one – Defining problems in terms of needs. After a successful set-up, moving directly to needs is advisable. Listing needs as they are expressed is helpful to stakeholders, as they can then track the Gordon sequence. A whiteboard or legal pad can be employed. (See the appendix). Avoid asking how parties *feel* about the problem. Such results in blame. Experienced facilitators know that listing needs in a non-judgmental fashion will allow deeper needs to flow to the surface.

Once listed, needs will invariably lend themselves to an *umbrella word or phrase* -- a condensation of several wants into a single all-encompassing need. Then an equation can be drawn so that the stakeholders can readily track the method. On the board, the facilitator can write: *How can we meet the needs of the employee (A) while also meeting the needs of the employer (B)?* Moving forward is simply a case of inserting the underlying needs. For example, on the Alaska/Halibut decision, the government's need to protect an endangered species was balanced with the boat crew's need to save lives. This problem contains a number of viable solutions.

(At this juncture, the concern is not with concealed needs or angry rebuttal. The object at this stage is to learn the Gordon sequence, and to do so as a neutral facilitator. Also, in order to focus on learning the steps, full and honest disclosure of the stakeholders is expected. More complicated collaborations will be discussed in chapter 3.)

The Cross-Check: Transitioning Step one to Step two. Before examining solutions, make sure both sides are invested in your process. In a real-time collaboration, if a crosscheck is not completed, one or both parties might revert to blaming. Blame is the last thing we need. Collaboration is a blame-free technique.

Check with stakeholders individually to see if they want to change their side of the equation. If not, keep moving forward -- make sure each 'side' understands the needs of the other. To complete the cross-check, ask the tell-all question: *Is it okay for 'Robert' to have the need(s) he expressed?* Failure to complete the crosscheck means the collaboration is at risk. Other than Gordon's redefining the problem, the crosscheck is the most vital part of the process. It is the reason, if any, for a collaborative endeavor falling through the cracks.

Step two – Searching for solutions. Once the crosscheck is complete, the facilitator can relax to an extent. Ideally, he or she can invite silly and even untenable solutions; laughter opens the mind to new ideas. Apart from the newness of the steps, this should be a stress-free time. Both sides are comfortable with the process, and the facilitator has kept them from opening a figurative door and dashing out. Each party has had the opportunity to disclose individual needs and honor the other person's need(s). By following the guidelines of brainstorming, they will search for solutions together. When one party offers a solution that largely meets the other person's need, the second person will often reciprocate. That is when the job of the facilitator is significantly, but not completely, done.

Step three -- Evaluating solutions. A successful collaboration should begin to crystallize a solution, and often in the interest of time, step #4 – choosing solutions – can automatically flow from step #2. If you find it necessary to evaluate ideas one at a time, try using the 'T' model that Benjamin Franklin introduced to chart financial accounts. This method takes longer, but because of its thoroughness, I prefer it in sticky situations.

To set up a 'T' chart for solution #1, head the left side with a minus sign and the right side with a plus. Now list limitations on the left and advantages on the right. Next do the same for solution #2, #3 and so on. When completed, a page full of T charts (and evaluations for each one) should result. You might have four advantages on the plus side and only one limitation, however that one disadvantage is a genuine liability to one party. So, you'll need to calibrate that in your outcome rather than simply count the number of advantages and the number of limitations. This method isolates, or flags, bad ideas. It also demonstrates that your stakeholders are working together to solve their problem.

Step four -- Choosing a solution. By this time in a collaboration, the truly satisfying solution will have bubbled to the surface. Often several ideas are acceptable to the stakeholders. Those can be combined. As will be seen in the examples that follow, numerous actions are worth pursuing at the same time.

Step five -- Implementing the solution(s). Not much needs to be said here except that *people who solve problems together implement solutions together.* That axiom applies to any group procedure. It simply reflects the truism that workers will do what *they* decide to do -- as far as doing what others decide? Not so much.

Shop owner Art Sabiston faced complications when his team repeatedly failed to clean up properly. After his collaboration ended, he wrote to me saying, "My men are cleaning without complaint since they had claimed ownership of the collaboration and accepted responsibility for cleaning relevant areas of the shop" (Sabiston, 2017, personal communication). As I like to say, once that point is reached, the Indians are side-by-side, (see the Crow ritual below).

Step six – Course Corrections/Follow-Up. A good idea from the start is to monitor progress as the stakeholders move forward implementing their solution. This can be on a daily or weekly basis, or it can mean simply reconvening at a later date. At that time, the team can modify its solution, pick another solution, or set a time for further evaluating what's being done. More will be said about follow-up in chapter three.

Historic Roots of Collaboration: The Crow Ritual

Native Americans lived in proximity, more so than we do in modern America. Tribes can be presumed to have councils and other means of settling problems. Some had elaborate rituals to celebrate peaceful methods, the following example coming from the Crow Nation (Personal communication through the Association of Experiential Education). It lends a kinetic element to my workshops and can be acted out at home or in the workplace. When enacted at home, the rite seems to find a comfortable place in family memories.

The Crow rite-of-passage was to initiate young people into tribal membership. With pre-teens waiting outside the tent or building, an elder would call one child into the tribe. There the juvenile would be told to face a second elder and join hands with this elder. Once joined at shoulder height, the two would be asked to push and shove without result. The presiding elder would ask the child, "Is that the way you want to solve problems with your brother?" Dutifully, the youngster would answer, "No."

The two would repeat the effort, but this time the elder would stumble reeling across the room. "Is that the way you want to solve problems?" "No."

Finally, when the youth shoved a third time, the elder would loop one hand over aikido style so that, hands still clenched, they are standing side by side. "Now where is your problem," the youngster is asked? Out in front. "Where is your vision?" Focused on the problem. "How are you standing?" Side by side. "Where are your shoulders?" They are touching, joined. Now the elder and the boy are shoulder-to-shoulder facing the symbol of their problem. Unfortunately, it is necessary to go back thousands of years to find a metaphor for collaborating, but there it is. The exercise can be viewed as both a look at Native American folklore and as a beginning for understanding collaboration.

Facilitating a Six-Step Process

To repeat, the Gordon method is best learned as a neutral facilitator. In this way students of collaboration can become comfortable applying the steps, not having to protect a need of their own. In fact, facilitating without that neutral third party is a difficult and often misunderstood process. A closer look at two-party collaboration will be found in chapter three. For now, three party facilitation is the rule – the facilitator and two others we will call stakeholders, or simply *parties* committed to solving a problem.

First, the facilitator introduces the process. This is the set-up mentioned above. State the purpose (so that both will win), confirm the time frame in two parts (It this a good time? Is it enough time?) and ask if the parties are willing to try something new.

Once permission to influence is achieved, go directly to needs. I recommend starting with the person who brought the problem to my attention. This is simply a good-will gesture allowing that person to feel their appeal is getting the consideration it deserves.

When listing needs, pay particular attention to notions the other party is likely to respect. Remember, the Cross-Check is within reach to get the parties side-by-side. But for now, only list the needs. You will want firm control of your process, and that is gained by guiding each step in sequence without letting one party or the other get ahead. The rule-of-thumb is this: It is okay to go backwards in the steps but not okay to forge ahead. This allows participants to modify their needs as they witness the collaborative effort helping their situation. It also lets the parties add solutions after step two is complete.

If one party gets ahead of the process, it is best to gently deflect their comment. When one person, say, offers a solution while I am still assessing needs, I say "I know you'd like to see this (or that) result. Remind me when we get to the step two. I will begin with your idea." This gentle handling of the disruption allows the facilitator to maintain a listening role while bringing the Gordon sequence back on line.

When assessing needs, pay particular attention to what I call "umbrella" statements – summaries that seem to encompass several needs. For example, in a sexually intimidating situation, your response, "You need to feel safe," will normally cover several needs – the need not to be hit upon, the need not to be teased, not to be threatened, etc. Umbrella phrases also fill in one side of the collaboration equation in a manner that is hard to rebut. The offender has to understand his victim's need to feel safe or he will oust himself from the process. *

Mutual understanding is completed with the cross-check, which is that important transition between steps one and two. Only when the cross-check is complete, when there is full acceptance of one another's needs, does solution finding come into play. Here the guidelines of brainstorming apply. At all costs, experienced mediators resist giving solutions. At this stage, the worst mistake facilitators can make is to give the best solution. Solving stakeholder's problems for them undermines ownership. It deflates the process in one innocent move. Besides, you may be surprised to learn you do not *have* the best solution.

*This applies to an early stage of discovery. If abuse can be *shown*, look for a legal solution.

As third-party facilitator, it is crucial to record key pieces of information: individual needs, the summary word (or phrase), the collaboration equation, solutions, evaluations, the eventual solution and assignments. The process ends when stakeholders agree on their assignment (or agree to continue their discussion later).

Here is one completed process submitted by a former student and another from the department of education.

Case Study:

"My name is Tim Warner, partner in a small sandwich shop we are trying to develop into a chain. We opened two new franchises in the past four months and are awaiting an investment decision on whether we can open one more. At this point, we are concerned that our customers experience a pleasant environment. We have been training employees in the manner of Starbucks to reach that goal.

"That said, we cannot afford to have two drivers fighting in a dispute over our routing system. I leapt from my office when I heard the commotion, 'You're pathetic!' shouted across the kitchen, separated from our customers by only a stand-alone counter. I told the two to follow me into the office and confronted them on their behavior. Dave is a youth right out of high school and Reggie is 60, retired. Reggie has accused other drivers of manipulating the routing computer. I asked him first what happened. He said Dave had done him a "favor" by letting him go first in the routine. When he got back from his run, he saw that Dave was on a delivery that took him to a customer well known for his tipping habits. "That should have been my run."

I told the men I had taken a class on problem-solving and asked if they wanted to try it out. Both shrugged. Under the circumstances, that was good enough for me. Next, I said there was one rule – that only one person could talk at a time. They reluctantly agreed (under duress). There was no question about time; I was going to keep them until we had things resolved.

Tim: "So Reg, what are the needs you have around delivery?"

Reggie: "I need to have my own routes. That computer is flawless. It is fair and it is always accessible, but not if someone abuses it under the guise of a 'favor.'

Dave: "What is he talking about, abuse?" (Talking over)

Reggie: "You know exactly . . ."

Tim: Reminding both about the angry rule.

Tim: OK Dave, what needs do you have?"

Dave: "I need to earn more money."

Tim: "More money?"

Dave: "Right. I'm back in college. I need to pay for my schooling."

Tim: "Doesn't Reggie need money too?"

Dave: "He doesn't need the money. He drives a Mercedes. Who delivers sandwiches in a Mercedes?"

Tim: "I'm going to let Reggie decide that."

Reggie: "I *don't* need the money. I need to stay active in retirement. Having some extra doesn't hurt. But most of all, I need that computer to be respected."

Tim: "I wonder if *you* need respect. . ."

Reggie: "Of course. This is about being manipulated"

Tim: (writing on a clipboard) "Let's try this out -- **How can we get Reggie the respect he needs so that Dave can save money for college, and I can focus on our expansion?**

Tim: "You guys see each other as the problem. The real problem is what I've just written.

Tim: "You've heard of brainstorming. Let's brainstorm now to see what solutions you can come up with to solve the larger problem."

Dave: "We can all get a raise.

Tim: Veto (laughter)! You just had a raise in January. The state took you to $14/hr.

Reggie: "We can give Dave more hours."

Dave: "We can shift one of us to a new store."

Tim: "More ideas?"

Reggie: "We can get hours for him at the new shops. Let him work both places."

Reggie: "But we need to stop toying with the computer. The computer is our boss."

Tim: "The drivers' boss."

Tim: "Should we fire a driver who manipulates the routing system?" (No answer)

"At this point, I felt we were getting adversarial, away from the spirit of the process. But we had a good equation and some effective solutions that would restore balance among our drivers. It has been our younger drivers who think they can defeat the system. Now they know that will have to go through a collaboration process, at the least, if they toy with the computer."

Second Case Study: This next case shows the depth of the stakes when one considers collaboration as an option.

The Problem; Debbi Wallace Report

"This collaboration takes place between Monica and Dylan, ten-year-olds in my fourth-grade classroom. They had been matched as partners for a cooperative learning activity. They were to choose a topic from the information on insects we'd been studying and present it to the class. They had been at a stalemate all morning as to how to present information on their chosen topic, 'How Crickets Sing.' They had asked for my help. I gave encouragement and suggested that they listen to each other's wishes. By 10 am, they were not talking at all.

"I perceived what I thought was their problem. Instead of telling them this time I decided it would be a great time to use my facilitator skills to help them discover each other's needs. The following is an overview of what took place.

The Set-Up

"I set things up informally as both agreed to use their library time to try this new process. They were apprehensive, but willing. We began with Monica stating her needs.

Trolling For Needs

"Monica needed to get the work done, to have it look good, not to have to do all the work and to have fun.

"Dylan needs were much slower in coming and difficult for him to state. He needed to get it done, not get in trouble, and not miss recess and to have help. At this point, I repeated Dylan's last comment to him. He said, 'Yes, it's too hard.' Monica reminded Dylan that he had agreed to the topic of crickets. 'I know but I don't want to write it.' I wrote that on his list: Dylan doesn't want to write.

"Dylan added, 'I can't read that stuff.' I asked if he needed help in reading and he said he did. I wrote 'help with reading.' By now, Monica's face was wide-eyed with surprise and Dylan was shifting in his chair.

"I introduced the needs equation. I reminded them that they would both be winners when we were done. Monica's side was easy for her to see. I led Dylan through a slow questioning process (which Monica listened to intently) and in the end he stated his own need. The equation looked like this – *How could we finish the project so that Monica doesn't have all the work and Dylan gets help and feels smart?*

"I checked with them, so they understood and accepted each other's need. Monica, especially, was very enthusiastic and supportive. 'I didn't know what you needed!' she grinned.

Possible Solutions

"From here things went quickly. They easily created a list of solutions, rejected a few and came up with a plan. I spoke only a word or two and they did the rest.

1. Get an adult to help
2. Use drawings/diagrams
3. Monica writes, and Dylan draws
4. Do a game show
5. Monica reads and Dylan picks important stuff to do (act out)
6. Make a video
7. Write a story about a cricket
8. Read together

Evaluating Solutions (Author's note; Debbi's report is shown verbatim. The children apparently evaluated their solutions by quickly throwing out those less plausible and combining the remaining four.)

Choosing The Solution

"Monica put their basic ideas into a (combined) plan involving solutions two, three, five and eight. They could draw pictures showing the information and write a sentence with each one, explaining what it means. Dylan added that he could act it out. 'It would be funny,' he said with a grin.

"I had them tell me what they thought they should do now. They decided to read the book at the same time and Monica would write down the important sentences. Dylan would draw diagrams to go with the sentences and they would color them together. Dylan also agreed to act out the part of a 'singing' cricket, much to Monica's relief! They both agreed to this solution and said they felt much better.

Implementing The Solution(s)

"That afternoon, they were talking and listening to each other. Monica was eager to help Dylan. He even had to back her off a bit. She asked for his opinion, and he offered to help in many ways. Smiles were plentiful.

A postscript from Debbi Wallace: "Dylan has a learning disability and reads at a low first grade level. He is learning to express his needs and to work through his difficulties, not ignore them. This was a giant step for him. Monica, obviously, had no idea about Dylan's weakness in reading. She is bright and sometimes quiet in new situations. If I had told them what they should do, Dylan wouldn't have communicated his needs and Monica would have missed out on the chance to understand."

One Note of Caution:

Debbi's job was to do more than guide the steps. She must take care to keep any aggressive remarks out of the needs assessment. She must translate whenever a need demands a change in the other stakeholder's behavior. So, for *Monica needs Dylan to help more,* Debbi would have written *Monica not have to do all the work.* Remember, it is Monica whose needs are being assessed. Likewise, among Dylan's needs -- for Monica to help with reading -- Debbi would note *for Dylan to get help with reading.* Using the passive voice to remain neutral is one key to success.

During the needs assessment, particularly in an adversarial situation, the person who feels aggrieved will often demand the other party do (or stop doing) certain behavior. If this is not corrected, it can lead back to bickering, reigniting the disagreement. It takes experience to catch these traps and disable them, but it is not hard to do. Simply keep names out of the picture. The facilitator simply changes to the passive voice. When a facilitator hears, "*To get Frank to stop fobbing his work off on me,* he or she will repeat, *"For you to quit doing another person's work."* This will almost certainly lead to the deeper need, "To concentrate of work of your own," and presto – you have a need the offender can sign off on. The idea is to get a *NEEDS EQUATION* that both parties can accept. The best way to do that is to quietly remove names from the assessment.

Summary

Any negotiation that seeks to balance underlying needs is a collaboration. Any discussion based on superficial wishes is a cooperative, not a collaboration. When learning to collaborate, look for an issue that can be resolved as a neutral third party and one where full disclosure is expected. This keeps inexperienced facilitators focused on the process and not on the behavior of the participants. Make sure to complete the critical junctures cleanly and clearly and try not to proceed without those. They are the Set-Up and the Cross-Check. In both cases, one's instincts will tell whether the stakeholders are invested and ready to move forward.

With that in mind, return to Gordon's six-step method. Go through the steps one at a time, allowing parties to go back to an earlier step, but not forward, getting ahead of the process. Control the collaboration; do not control the people. For example, say, "Thanks. We will evaluate solutions when we get more ideas on the board. Meantime, hold that thought. We'll need it when we measure your ideas."

Translate aggressive comments so that they become inoffensive to the opposing party. Simply change to the passive voice. This is easily done by keeping names out of the assessment. Get closure to each process or be exact about when it will continue. Get commitment to the solution from stakeholders along with roles to be played when implementing the new idea(s).

Leaders are changing the power balance in their spheres of influence. They are demonstrating the truth that *to surrender power is to gain power.* They are finding workers at peace with one another, eager for collaborating to work, and pleased with the results.

Chapter 3

Advanced Collaboration

"First Your Pants, Then Your Shoes"
Gary Larson, The Far Side

If you thought collaboration's six-step process mirrors conflict resolution, you would be correct. However, many who study conflict are dismayed to learn how hard it is to deal with, especially when they are part of the dispute. For the most part, conflict resolution workshops demonstrate that resolution is *possible*. However, the art and science of conflict resolution is best left to the experts. Unless, of course, conflict resolution is taught as a special case of collaboration. In that event, it is simply an aftermarket bolt-on to the basic design.

Imagine a stream running along a map until it reaches a bridge. But the bridge, symbolizing conflict, is destroyed and has fallen into the water to block traffic. That bridge defines conflict. Now imagine that upstream of the damage, there lies conflict resolution. Upstream of that lies conflict *prevention* and still farther upstream one finds problem solving. Further upstream of problem solving is problem prevention and further than that, routine decision-making. The purpose of chapter two has been to introduce problem solving along the collaborative model, but also to enable leaders to adopt a vocabulary that focuses on human needs. As such, the previous chapter provides a structure for ordinary deciding. Safety of individual staff members, particularly emotional safety, depends on this type of teaming. Fundamental to the desired context is to negotiate over the shared problem and never over entrenched positions (Fisher and Ury, 1981, p. 38).

With this in mind, we will examine what happens to the collaborative moment when parties will not reveal their needs. Other advanced scenarios occur when the collaborating parties are hostile, when there is anger and hidden agenda both, and when there are multiple parties to the collaboration. Add to these, difficult moments when there is no neutral person to facilitate. Here, the skilled party must protect her/his needs while also guiding the process. The schematic shown below illustrates how developmental training proceeds when we have a neutral facilitator (F). Bear in mind, if either party is unwilling to take part in your collaboration, you have twenty-three alternate leader styles to choose from. (Chapter 4)

COLLABORATING WITH HIDDEN NEEDS

Throughout chapter two, we have assumed full disclosure from A and B. More than that, we have assumed novice collaborators will first attempt the Gordon process as a neutral architect. This allows them to be uninterested in outcomes and able to focus on the problem-solving sequence. The next development would be facilitating when the parties do not reveal their needs. This is represented by the dotted line connecting A and B (below).

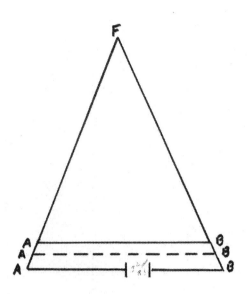

This shows the training module or design. With this in mind, we will examine what happens to the collaboration when stakeholders are not forthcoming.

The purpose of collaborating amid hidden needs is to dredge up such needs to where they can be winnowed into the collaborative equation. Recall from the previous chapter that needs start out as basic to human existence, then become more sublime as one progresses through life. Unmet needs, then, dictate where parties A and B are entering the process. The way to bring them into play is to listen. Active listening means hearing what is said and communicating to participants that they are being attended to, in other words, heard. Teachers, thanks to training and decades of emphatic practice, are adept at active listening. They use it every day. They have taught Millennial children how to listen, perhaps not as directly as in the Gordon method. Their teaching is by example, and it is constant. Listening engenders trust in the process -- equally important when uncovering hidden needs. Listen effectively and you will get buy-in for your process.

I am indebted to consultant David Landsburg of Tucson, Arizona for his *NON-DIRECTIVE LISTENING FOR MANAGERS*, the most succinct short form of instruction I am aware of. Below is the Landsburg handout, inserted here with permission.

Non-Directive Listening for Managers

Research studies suggest that the number one subordinate complaint about managers is that they do not listen. Part of the reason for those findings is that, indeed, managers may not listen enough. Another part of the reason is that managers may not give enough feedback to their employees indicating that they are trying to listen.

Carl Rogers developed a counseling technique which is called either "Active Listening" or "Non-directive listening." It is based on the concept that a counselor or psychologist can help a client solve his problem by listening to him in a non-directive manner. This same approach can be used by managers to help employees solve their own problems. Such a practice encourages personal growth on the part of employees. It also means that employees are more apt to buy into the solution, since they developed it themselves.

Rules

The following list of six rules gives a basic overview of the non-directive listening process.

1. **Take time** to listen carefully. Non-directive listening cannot be hurried. If you have an important appointment in a few minutes, do not start non-directive listening. Instead, set an appointment to deal with the problem at a later time.

2. **Be attentive** to the employee. Concentrate your total attention on what the employee is saying.

3. **Give three verbal reactions.** Those reactions are all designed to show the employee that you are trying to understand what is being said. Yet, you do not want to direct the conversation. The reactions are silence (the employee will usually fill the silence by telling you more), intelligent grunts (such as "uh huh") which say I understand, but still do not direct the conversation, and paraphrasing, which involves repeating what you heard in terms of both content and feelings.

4. **Use no aggressive probes.** Your natural curiosity will often cause you to want to ask specific questions to get more information. However, that makes you the director and reduces the probability that the employee will solve the problem himself.

5. **Never evaluate** what the employee is telling you. You do not disagree with him. Nor, do you say you support his opinion. Employees will often want your opinion. However, if you give

Rev. Don Broadwell

them an opinion, you begin to direct them in the problem solving
process. This may not be in their best interest.

6. **Never lose faith** in the ability of the employee to solve
the problem. The principle on which this system works is that
people can solve their own problems. By solving the problem
herself, the employee becomes more committed to making the
solution work, and at the same time develops problem solving
skills.

The underlying principle is that the manager should give
lots of feedback which says to the employee that "I really want
to understand what you are saying."

<u>When to Use</u>

Using this technique will get you high marks from employees
who want their managers to listen to them more. It might also
improve employee commitment to the task. However, the total
technique cannot be used in all situations. Consider the
following four factors when deciding whether or not to use non-
directive listening in any specific situation.

1. Confirm that you are discussing a complex problem. It is
probably not worth getting into the process if the employee just
wants to know whether to use form A or form B.

2. Make certain you have the necessary time and commitment
to go through the process. It is not wise to start the non-
directive listening process, only to cut the conversation short
to move on to a more important matter.

3. Be sure that you can withhold judgement on the issue. It
is admirable to help employees in solving problems. However, you
must be able to live with whatever solution is selected. If the
employee is trying to decide whether or not it is appropriate to
drink alcohol at lunch time, there may be company policy which
already makes the decision.

4. Only use the process in proportion. Employees will grow
very tired of intelligent grunts and nodding silence if you use
the technique all the time.

Americans are feeling increasingly alienated -- from
neighbors, from families, from companies. People are looking for
someone who will listen to them -- someone to whom they can be
committed. By using some portion or all of the process of non-
directive listening, you can help employees solve their own
problems, increase their commitment to the company and increase
their commitment to you as a manager.

Incidentally, the same principles work for salespeople,
especially during the interview phase when you are trying to
discover the customer's felt needs.

 DAVID L.
LANDSBURG
(602) 885-1602

9160 E. Holmes • Tucson, Arizona #5710

One technique missing from Landsburg's approach is another
device for encouraging participants to open up – it is the upward
inflection of the spoken word. This indicates that one is asking a
question. Effective facilitators will choose a key word (or phrase) and
simply repeat it with an upward inflection. For example, one party
to the collaborative might say, "I didn't know it was that far away."
Try saying, "That far away?" "Yes, because it will take me longer

to get there." "Take longer?" "I can't get away early. I'm afraid I'll walk in late."

People enjoy being attended to. This simple exercise helps them get in touch with hidden needs, then articulate them to the facilitator. It also builds trust, both in the facilitator and the process. Of course, one might say, "Tell me more about that . . . ", or "Say more on that. . . "Still, as indicated by Landsburg's heading, active listening tends to be non-directive. On the other hand, a steady diet of listening can irritate. So be ready to alternate using the direct approach. Just know that you are there to build trust. And remember, your purpose from the beginning is to see that both sides win.

AN EXAMPLE OF FACILITATING WITH UNSPOKEN NEEDS

A local Kiwanis club was a week away from installing new officers when the outgoing and incoming presidents, together with myself, were caucusing to develop fresh ideas. The new president -- I'll call him Allen -- suggested changing the first meeting of the month to a general meeting rather than a director's meeting, as had been the long-standing tradition. This meant coming up with a schedule for board meetings outside the accepted monthly practice. The old president we'll call Fred.

Fred: "I can tell you, I'd be against a change like that."
Allen: "Why? I want to give that first monthly meeting back to the general membership."
Fred: "I'm just against it. I see no reason for the change."
Me: (after a few minutes of the same) "Would you guys' mind if I facilitated here?" I went through the checklist for opening a collaboration, ending with my purpose to see that both men would win. They agreed.

Me: "Allen, what are your needs around shifting that first meeting over to the members?"

Allen: "Meetings are fun. I want to share them with the rest, like every week."

Me: "What does it do for you to extend that initial meeting to everybody?"

Allan: "I don't know."

Me: "What would it be if you did know?" (Another gambit on my part)

Allen: "I'm not sure." (Gambit failed)

Me: "Fred, what do you need around these meetings?"

Fred: "I need things to stay the way they are."

Me: "You're content with the status quo."

Fred: "Well, sure. I can't come to a separate board meeting no matter when."

Me: "Can't come?"

Fred: "I travel farthest anyway. I just can't add one more meeting."

Me: "So it's economical – only travel to three meeting a month plus one board meeting."

Fred: "Yes."

Me: "Let's enter that in the collaboration equation – Fred needs to minimize his travels.

Allen, have you identified your need around changing it up?"

Allen: "I think I would like to identify myself as caring about the membership, about making a decision that favors their interests."

Me: "We can enter that. But it seems as if we have a third party to these deliberations. Do we know what members want?"

Fred: "I don't know of any dissatisfaction with the way things are. Why not see what the members want?"

At this point, we agreed to the collaboration equation – HOW CAN WE meet Fred's need to economize his travel SO THAT we meet Allen's need for acting in favor of the group? Next on our agenda would be to raise the question in front of the membership. [In fact, private conversations showed no one wanted four open meetings. The issue was dropped, saving Allen from raising a question he could not pursue.]

COLLABORATING WITH ANGRY PEOPLE

With the way Allen and Fred started out, I feel sure things would have disintegrated. Fred already had dug in his heels with, "If you change the board meeting, I won't come to it." Allen had frustrated both Fred and I for being slow to identify his need. But what do facilitators do when issues become heated?

COLLABORATING WHEN ANGER IS PRESENT

Let's look back for a moment. In your set-up, you will need to add a cautionary word if anger is anticipated. This is the one rule that governs collaboration; there are no others. *Only one person can talk at a time.* I call this The Angry Rule, and my suggestion is not to invoke it if aggressive feelings are not present. My reasoning is people are hounded by enough rules. They can more easily open up if they are free of them, if just for the moment. Once again, The Angry Rule is part of the set-up, and only needs mention if anger is on the horizon. [Facilitating amid anger is symbolized by the communication blockage between A and B in the diagram (page 45). F continues as the neutral third party.]

By this time in the incremental sequence, we are at conflict resolution, but we have arrived by quite a different route. By treating con-res as a special case of collaboration, we can assume there is an overlay of skilled communication in place in your workplace or building. This makes resolving conflict one of the easiest of problems to resolve. Three reasons for this are, 1) employees are comfortable with the collaborative overlay, and are eager to reinforce it, 2) despite the urban myth that people like to fight, they actually like resolution, and 3) angry people will tell you what they need. You will simply need a recipe for turning the anger around to where it works in your favor. Before you do that, you can profit from what every professional counselor has carved in stone on her desk – ***Hear the feelings first!*** Let's go to an example.

Volleyball coach Steven Johnson describes what happens when conflict erupts between two women, affecting the performance of his team. Normally, Nikki and Tonya are friends, having played together for years. Here is Steven's report.

"When catty remarks occurred in the past, and with time at a premium, I would attempt to solve the problem using an authoritarian approach, 'All right ladies, what's the problem? Here is the solution, now get back to practice."

"Thirty minutes into practice, Nikki said, 'You could have gotten that ball if you would just move your feet.'

"INTRODUCTION: "I called Tonya and Nikki over and expressed my concern about the friction that was developing between them, and that I wanted to help them both have their needs met. When I asked if it was a good time, both girls said no; they wanted to keep on with practice but could stay after long enough to resolve the issue.

"After practice I repeated my concern and asked if they were willing to try a new method that will allow them both to get their needs met. They agreed. I then told them that in order for the process to work, only one person can talk at a time. Again, they both agreed.

Steven: "Tonya, let's begin with you. What are your needs?"
Tonya: (Animated) "I need the coach to provide feedback, not Nikki"
Steven: "You feel strongly that I'm the one to give any criticism."
Tonya: "Yes. And I need Nikki to treat me with respect."

Nikki: (Talking over) "But how can I respect you if you don't support me in the games?"

Steven: (With hand up to Nikki) "Nikki, remember. We'll get to your needs in a moment."

Nikki: (Nods)

Steven: (To Tonya) "It's respect then, isn't it? You need to be respected on the floor."

Tonya: "Not just in volleyball, all the time."

Steven: "I understand."

I then asked Nikki to consider her needs.

Nikki: "I need Tonya to help me in games and in practice."

Steven: 'You need to be supported."

Nikki: "Yes, and I need Tonya to give me a chance to give input when the team is in a huddle."

Steven: "Input in the huddle?"

Nikki: "Yes. You know when we huddle up. That's when Tonya cuts me off. She has a bad habit."

Steven: "So it happens regularly. And that makes you mad."

Nikki: "Well, sure."

Steven: "Do I understand, Nikki, that you need support from the team and to help with input in the huddle?"

Nikki concurred. I then asked Tonya if she understood what Nikki was saying and if it was okay for her to take that stance?

Tonya: "I understand. It is okay."

Steven: (Turning to Tonya) "And do I understand that I am the only one to give coaching feedback?"

"I turned to Nikki and asked if she understood what Tonya was saying and was it okay? Nikki understood and said O.K.

Steven: "So how can Nikki feel free to give input to the team and receive verbal support for her efforts so that Tonya can feel free of peer criticism and be respected?" Once both women acknowledged their needs were valid, the brainstorming process began. Alternating, Nikki and Tonya offered solutions.

Nikki's solutions: Not to coach Tonya

To support Tonya's efforts and suggestions

To have she and Tonya pair up during partner drills

Tonya's solutions: Not to speak in team huddles until everyone has a chance to talk

To verbally encourage the team during practice and games

The two agreed that they wanted to implement all the solutions. They understood my wanting to pair them up only sometimes out of concern for the interaction that occurs among the team. They agreed to meet one week later to assess how their solutions were working and if any adjustments need to be made.

CONCLUSION – Steven J.

"Since taking Don's class and implementing the principles with Nikki and Tonya I can now see that the authoritarian approach is counterproductive and negatively impacts team chemistry. By facilitating the process, the women were able to communicate their needs with a neutral party and have them validated by the other person. I was surprised they didn't come up with solutions that the other would find disagreeable. However, after giving the process some thought, I concluded that the solutions suggested were reasonable and accepted because the girls first acknowledged the other's needs. Finally, my stress level remains low as the participants become the problem solvers."

THE ORIGIN OF ANGRY FEELINGS

What makes a person angry? He or she has suffered loss. Here is where you make anger work in your favor. Angry people will tell you about their loss; *there you have their gain.* Presto! You already have one side of the equation. By settling feelings, you will have brought the parties to where they can be assertive with each other.

Aggressiveness does hinder communication, at least until a facilitator intervenes to hear the hurt, resolve it and uncover the underlying need. Think of it this way; Aggressive behavior says, "You're stupid." Passive behavior implies, "I'm stupid." Think of assertive behavior as neither passive nor aggressive. Forget the rulebook on how to assert oneself. Simply translate B's aggression into words which A can accept. One way to do this, as mentioned above, is to change from the active to the passive voice. For example, when John says, "Sandra keeps disciplining me in front of the others," your response can be, "You don't like being rebuked in public." Shifting to the passive voice keeps Sandra's name out of the picture temporarily, long enough for her to sit still with your statement. Remember, if Sandra erupts, remind her that only one person can talk at a time.

Enforcing The Angry Rule can be as light as a gentle hand facing the offending party. Equally, you can remind A about rule, saying "I can't help you if both talk at the same time," or threatening to abort the process if the disruption continues. Finally, asking, "What would you like to have happen now?" will really turn up the spotlight on any obstructionists. Facilitators occupy a powerful position in the collaboration. Parties A and B do not want that power; it means the end of problem solving. I have seen situations where the disputants willingly give power back to their facilitator, and I have even experienced it in a life-threatening moment in my own life.

Years ago, I was jogging on Seattle's Queen Anne Hill when a youngster lying flat on his skateboard went flashing down through traffic, narrowly missing a car turning into his path. I instinctively grasped the arm of one of his less foolish friends as he tramped past, with, "Hey! Your friend could have been killed." The young man jerked his arm away and when I reached the bottom of the hill, three of them blocked me into a dead-end corner of a park. No one was there to witness as they jabbed their boards within inches of my face, threatening to kill me if I touched one of them again.

Foolishly, I tried to tough the moment out. I remembered

a movie line Gene Hackman used to get out of a tight spot. I confronted the talker, "You got a pretty good attorney?" "Yeah," he barked, "I got three of them and they just got me out. Same as they'll do next time."

I couldn't dig myself in any deeper, so I went belly up. I sat on a rock abutment. They mustn't see my knees shaking. "*What do you want to happen now?*" The situation immediately evaporated! Their leader backed off, lowering his board. The others did the same, while chiming in absent mindedly, "We'll get you old man," and "Don't you worry." They strode away, leaving me a confused bundle of nerves. (And I was not *that* old.)

The truth of the matter is this: your conflict resolution will never get as far as my misadventure so long as you introduce the collaborative overlay in your workplace. In chapter 4, we will look at any number of interventions that can exist side-by-side with collaboration. In the meantime, know that collaborating using a neutral third-party facilitator is the last, best place for those involved in a dispute. This is even truer when employees are known to collaborate and do so in smaller ways every day. By this time in your journey, everyone is watching.

COLLABORATING WITHOUT A THIRD-PARTY FACILITATOR

Guiding a collaboration while 'owning' part of the problem is hard. Nevertheless, experienced facilitators – those who have perhaps profited from their experience as a neutral party – will find they can conquer the challenge with a modicum of difficulty. The schematic below shows what this facilitation looks like, moving from full disclosure through hidden agenda and ending with conflict. Note how the skilled party shifts (F). This illustrates a point, any stakeholder can facilitate, provided he/she is willing and has the skills.

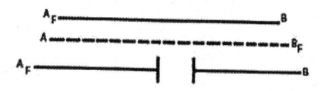

SIDEBAR

This diagram shows the more advanced training model where an neutral facilitator is not present.The role of 'F' must be played by the party with skill in that area,either A or B. Once again,training in collaboration is designed to be incremental,developmental.

THis normally requires practice as a third party facilitator.It is a difficult way to learn because one's counterpart to the collaboration might view neutral behavior as a weakness.'Changing hats' as Gordon called it is neither for the timid nor for the beginner

This paper was prepared by Amir Chakraborty, a former student. At the time of his writing, Amir was working part-time at a small computer shop. He had the unusual experience reported below.

"On the day in question, I was working my store when I heard shouting coming from the check-out line. My owner, who happened to be staffing the till, was engaged with a customer who wanted to return a power unit that was 31 days out, or one day past the return point, which is 30 days. Their conversation was heated. The customer refused to understand why he was being denied consideration as his late time was only one day. My owner was insistent on the letter of the law.

"I interrupted their dispute to say I had taken a class on problem-solving (I avoided saying it was on *leadership*) and I would like an opportunity to fix it so both sides could feel a win. Time constraints were obvious as there were customers in the queue, but I did mention that only one person could speak at a time. Surprisingly, both agreed. The other customers seemed amused but were likewise agreeable to the delay. I proceeded without asking if the principals were willing. It seemed unnecessary since I already had their attention.

"I started with the returning buyer, who said he needed to get his money back. My owner said he needed to enforce the rules about returns. I tried to address their feelings and had success in quieting down the argument. But the equation they had was not negotiable according to the way I learned to collaborate. I asked what it would mean if each could have their way, and we got to an equation that was workable – How can we have the owner remain in business so that the customer could complete his project on budget? They immediately signed off on a store credit. The way they came to this agreement meant most to the owner, as signified by the respect he got from shoppers in the queue. The returning buyer was also satisfied. Altogether it was good PR for the store and good customer relations for all sides.

Summary

Stepping directly into a conflict, attempting to resolve it without the backdrop of a collaborative culture, is a challenge. Still, conflict resolution is just one of four subsets of collaboration. The other three are hidden needs, collaborating without a skilled (neutral) facilitator, and collaborating among many and varied personalities, each with their own set of desires. This is why it becomes something of an imperative to establish a collaborative culture in your workplace. Your employees will quickly learn what can and cannot be negotiable under the collaborative overlay. Equally important, they will learn behaviors expected of them under twenty-four different problem-solving styles.

Millennials are adept at speaking their mind. Equally important, they are sensitive to belong to something greater than themselves. They need employers who can be ringmasters, organizing and shaping input so that it contributes to productivity as well as the welfare of the group. In the next chapter, we will examine Bi-Polar leadership and how some two dozen leader styles fit beside the collaborative model. This means abandoning the Industrial Hierarchy, replacing it with a linear spectrum as will be seen in chapter four.

Chapter 4

Situational Leadership Revised

~~~

"I was an oak. Now I'm a willow. I can bend."
Elvis Presley

Two questions hang over the collaboration debate. The first, is collaboration the paradigm that engages Millennials, that brings out the best in them and in their work? And second, what happens when collaboration meets an established leader design like Hersey/ Blanchard's Situational Leadership, that is, leading that fluctuates depending on maturity of the group? We will soon see that collaborative leadership leans on external measures, not just those inside the group. First however, we must examine the culture surrounding us, which is far from collaborative as it stands.

Lao Tzu was no clairvoyant. When he declared, "The leader is best when people barely know he exists" (Heider, 1986), the ancient sage could not have seen the appearance of American culture in our time. A tone of hostility and angst mark public exchange. We recently survived four years indulging an intimidator at the highest office in the land. Right wing media spews exaggeration and inuendo and citizens make New York cab drivers seem like choir boys. Aggression hovers. In places of civic discourse, normally where problems get solved, Roberts Rules is the best we can do; a win-lose posture governs exchange. Neither Roberts Rules nor adversarial voting addresses relationships. Debate is oriented around content only. As a result, the prevailing wisdom states that "people need to be commanded and controlled and that leaders need to be strong and have the right answers" (Straus, 2002, p. 186). Worse, Margaret Thatcher's enigmatic *Consensus is the negation of leadership* has enough devotees to steer collaboration straight into the jaws of conflict (Thatcher, 2004).

Today, leaders find themselves with bullseyes on their backs and leadership as dizzying a task as they have faced. Hubris notwithstanding, the dean at a prominent northwest university solves his dilemma this way: "There is one way to lead around here. Mine!" (Personal communication of January 2017)

Leadership! Socrates had trouble with it. So too, did Trump. If you're an employer, here is what to expect from Millennials -- the dominant generation in your workforce. (Fry, R., Pew Research, April. 2018). For starters, let's acknowledge that Millennials are not operating in their father's workplace. Work has become increasingly flexible, virtual and distributed, which means that self-management is more important than ever (Congleton, C., and Heikkinen, K., Entrepeneur. com, August 2017). To the contrary, detractors of Millennials say they are overconfident, opinionated, ambitious, entitled, and demanding.

- Demanding. Millennials have yet to learn the fine art of the request.
- Overconfident. "Millennials tend to overestimate their abilities and knowledge, which is especially irritating to older generations who have spent far more years on the job" (entrepreneur.com/article/301069). They must be attended to as well.
- Entitled, demanding. "Millennials are notoriously difficult to retain. Research from Gallup shows they are the least engaged generation at work and are three times as likely

to change jobs as non-millennials. The cost of millennial turnover in the U.S. is an estimated 30 billion dollars each year" (entrepreneur.com/article/301069)

"As employers strive to remain competitive, they will need to cultivate a work environment that allows for greater freedom and collaboration, manages concerns around job security and provides opportunities for meaningful work" (NA, ADP.com, Jan. 2021).

Watch what happens to one leader who couldn't adjust in the interim between two of her assignments. School principal Gerri Harmon was prudent about her new job -- *Be decisive right from the start.* She paced her campus, and then cut fifteen minutes off the working day. Were her teachers impressed? They filed a grievance overnight. "What's the difference, she grimaces, I'm doing what I did at my last school. These people will not let me take charge" (Personal communication, 2018).

Today there are many reasons why leading is different. Some-- self-esteem training, assertiveness and empowerment -- were put in place during Millennials' schooling (and which now apply to Gen Z and Generation Alpha). As ironic as it is fitting, Harmon must oversee the boisterous free-for-all which results. A single reason, however, stands above the rest. In the years since Harmon passed a similar initiation in a nearby district, the hierarchy has flattened. Corporate America manipulated the flattening by cutting venues, slashing middle managers, and plowing savings into The Bottom Line. For Harmon, this progression does not exist. For Harmon, a flattened hierarchy means more than truncated chains of command. It means, suitably enough, that authority-for-authority's sake is dead. With independent expression encouraged, educators must listen, harmonize and synthesize, all without resorting to power. Until we learn to do this, workers will continue to thrust ideas, but with little respect for the other guy's ideas. So, while nobody wants to be the leader, everyone wants to act like they're in the lead.

Face-to-face with Harmon, and with no glib fix in mind, I stalled. "You're hurt by this lack of support," I stumbled. "Well, of course!" An anguished look spread over Harmon's cautious decorum.

"I don't want control all the time," she pleaded, "I just want some control some of the time" (Personal communication, 2016). With hierarchical models breaking down, many employers feel the same as Harmon. When do they need control and how much control do they need? Bart Simpson comes alive in every factory and shop. Leaders must dance to his tune, balancing command-and-control with respect for the verbosity of every worker.

Hersey/Blanchard: The Reigning Standard

For fifty years, merging authority with supportive decision-making has been the domain of Paul Hersey and Ken Blanchard, originators of a bell curve they named Situational Leadership. Hersey/Blanchard argued that traditional leading, based on codes of accountability and the power to punish and reward, can be adjusted according to stages of group cohesion. As shown in Figure #1 (counterclockwise from bottom right), the situational leader directs less as the subordinate group matures (Hersey, 1984).

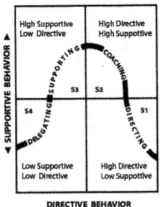

from bottom right), the situational leader decides less as the subordinate group matures (Hersey, 1984).

THE FOUR LEADERSHIP STYLES

Figure 1 Source: Hersey, P.

Situational leadership can be readily applied. At many universities, Hersey/Blanchard permeates training for managers. Small business would seem an ideal incubator for Hersey/ Blanchard. In many cases it is. Yet like the leading it promotes, Situational Leadership itself can be modified, adjusted to meet modern realities.

Hersey/Blanchard rests on internal measures – trust, bonding, knowledge, industry, and heart. Today, we can amplify Hersey/ Blanchard so that it recognizes forces acting *upon* the group as well as those within. In today's cubicles, internal measures are not enough. Neither is it acceptable for leaders to subjectively assess their group's maturity. This definitive quality of leadership is what grates. Needed is a way to balance authority with participation, to blend collaborative leading with command-and-control. Yet as Jurist Michael Josephson years ago lamented, "We stubbornly try to force authority to make some compromise with participation, and without success" (Josephson with Bill Moyers, 1988).

Situational Leadership Revisited

What happens when we chart leadership not according to group development, rather by the number of people who decide? If we accept Thomas Gordon's thesis that the terms leadership and problem-solving are interchangeable, we pop through Alice's rabbit lair into uncharted landscapes indeed (Gordon, 1977: p 27). Just as there are many ways to solve problems, there are many ways to lead.

To match leader methods to events in the workplace, first create a spectrum, or 'menu' of styles (Figure 2). Compromising, voting, commanding, and consulting are all traditional methods for deciding. Collaborating is innovative. Authority serves as the pole on the left. One hundred percent participation (for example, jury deliberations, becomes the pole on the right.)

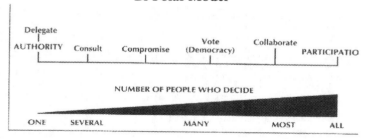

Figure 2 Source: The Author

By arranging leader interventions along the resulting chart, leaders can adjust their style to match events. Their behavior then flexes with circumstances, perhaps shifting so rapidly that methods appear to overlap. Teacher Mary Shaw, for example, returned from recess to shouts from every fourth grader in her class (personal communication, 2013). The use of the school basketball had triggered a dispute with another class. Mary opened the divider between classes (decided) supervised the choice of speakers (appointed), and then facilitated (collaborated) between factions. The two classes not only spoke through their delegates (representative democracy), but they also caucused (consulted) at times among themselves. Practiced Bi-Polar Leaders not only recognize these shifts, they foster them – and begin the delicate balance of participation with command-and-control.

The Role of Personal Values

Before leaders can adopt such a variable model, a refresher in facilitation skills will help. However, they face a more daunting task – defining their essence as leaders. Faced with a multifaceted approach, leaders can profit by determining which styles are compatible with their own mindsets and goals. As never before, they need to be clear about personal values. Since every employer will have unique values, personal menus will differ, becoming exclusive to the character and goals of each woman or man. While this precludes a universal leader template, it also requires leaders to develop their own templates. Unlike the boss who stands on authority, today's managers must do nothing less than uncover and honor their own uniqueness. Ask yourself, "What's important to me as I lead others?" Then start your list.

To be proactive when choosing a style, managers must tighten the grip on their values. For them to be recognized according to their dynamic along the chart (as opposed to how they wield power), they need to put aside appearances and allow themselves to be known. Most will be content with five or six favored interventions. Research among Millennials shows once the menu pattern of the leader is recognized, energy and enthusiasm infuse the office, the cubicles, and even the factory floor.

Key Indicators: Impact and Concern

To guide variable leading among in-touch and vocal millennials, leaders will serve their interests by including one set of measures not found in Hersey/Blanchard – impact and concern. After decades of uneven renewal, impact and concern remain the hot buttons in the workplace. When pushed, they inflame entire communities, especially when decisions roll down from the top. These are the *hit* and *hurt* of modern leading. Impact and concern will continue to transform leadership. These two factors clamor for attention when decisions are made across the land. For example, to the question of who shall decide, we might ask: Who is affected? Who cares? Who has information we need? What degree of trust exists among the group? What priorities need attention? How much time do we have? Reformers like Warren Bennis agree: To accomplish such alchemy, effective leadership begs to consider the concerns of employees who put decisions to work. When leaders address these measures, the scope of their leading changes. The question is no longer how much authority to use; rather, should authority be used at all?

Selecting a style

With two dozen problem-solving methods from which to choose, how shall I intervene? This question divides leadership into a two-step sequence. Leaders will first determine how a decision will be reached. Because bi-polar leading affects buy-in, matching style with events is more important than the wisdom of the actual decision. This example is another way of saying that what is decided is not as important as employees accepting the solution and putting their shoulders to the wheel. Even Machiavelli knew "leaders must carefully analyze and understand the context for leadership before acting. He knew that leaders must have a range of leadership practices in their repertoire and must choose those practices that are most likely to achieve results in a particular situation" (Chrislip, & Larson, 1994, p. 55)

In the figure on page 65, leaders can select not from one style (authority), but from seven styles -- two based in authority and others in some form of participation. Since authority-based leading involves one decision maker, the diagram shows authority on the left. Increasing the number of deciders moves the reader's imagination to the right. Of the disciplines shown, five are traditional. Pure participation is vague and as such, problematic. Collaborative leading, despite much rhetoric, remains innovative. Because it has the structure lacking in random participation, collaborating becomes the *operative* pole on the right. Adding styles completes the framework, a menu arranged by the number of people who decide.

Some styles are harder to place than others. Collaboration, for example, might be placed anywhere except at the pole on the left. In general, collaboration is a peer model of deciding, shunning authority, and rank. Sometimes confused with collegiality or consensus, it is a process for *reaching* consensus. In general, two people can collaborate.

So can an entire department. Since many individuals might be involved, collaboration is shown nearer the pole on the right.

Once collaboration is decided upon, the leader/facilitator will begin to involve workers. Are employees affected? Are they concerned? Do they have information the leader needs? Do they want a voice? Can stakeholders trust the others? Do they trust their leader? Or does the leader already have a solution in mind? Predetermined solutions spell trouble for would-be collaborators. Leaders who obscure their decision-making while mouthing the jargon of collaboration have difficulty without equal, even among raw authoritarians. They place themselves at a high-risk position – top left along the chart.

Trust for the Process

Trust for the process might come slowly. Where trust is present, workers eagerly share their solutions and ideas. Employees quickly sense when to speak up, how to stay within the boundaries of each style, and when they are legitimately excluded from debate. Wonderfully prepared by decades of classroom innovation -- training in assertiveness, listening, and self-esteem – Millennials are ideally suited for the features of the Bi-Polar chart. When leaders use the model, the model itself generates trust. Trust increases regard for the model, resulting in reciprocity, just as with any mutual connection. Two years into Bi-Polar leading, school principal Lynn Roberts was astonished when two teachers asked to combine their curricula. "These two weren't speaking with one another before we adopted the new model." (Roberts, personal communication, 2018). Different leaders find different rewards. Flexible leading gives vice principal and school counselor Katherine Palmer an uncommon bonus – confidence. "I found a way to blend my two roles. It's okay to move from one end of the chart to the other. It's under my control."

(Palmer, personal communication, 2020). Beyond shifting among styles, it is during implementing where miracles seem commonplace. In the classroom, teacher Raymond Salinas's collaboration resulted in students generating their own criteria for grading group presentations. Salinas reports: "It's been a couple of days since my students devised their plan and implemented it. Watching my students has been refreshing. I see them working harder than normal, being more responsible for their learning and having a better attitude for their work. Also, that work is much better than what it had been before. I notice a sense of pride. (Salinas, personal communication, 2020). Teachers like Salinas do more than guide effective solutions. They transform the construct of power in the workplace and provide a framework to resolve problems in the future. For employees to become effective leaders themselves, they need exposure to many leader styles. By demonstrating from among some two dozen interventions (Fig 3), leaders can show a reasonable complement of methods without surrendering authority altogether.

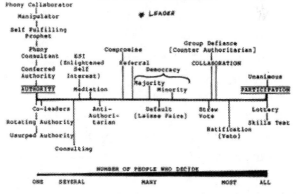

SITUATIONAL LEADERSHIP MENU
BI-POLAR MODEL

Indexing to one allows that authority-based leading has its place. Leaders reluctant to share power have their own integrity; they simply have different values. With bi-polar leading, no employer needs to change. However, for men and women comfortable with authority, that fact may be best acknowledged. In today's world, acknowledging the tendency toward command-and-control may take more daring than learning new styles. Even so, as renowned scholar Abraham Maslow has written, "Many people assume that power in the form of strong leadership is always bad, overlooking the fact that there are healthy leaders whose motives are for the good of their organizations and for the good of society" (Goble, 2004: p. 97). So, which will it be – authority-based leading or group-based leading? For decades, leaders have appeared in limbo between the two, frustrating change and limiting reform.

The Not-So-Democratic Vote

As surreal as it seems, virtually all managers already use a twin-poled model. However, the pole on the right is the democratic vote. Voting fails the participation test for three reasons. First, it favors those who are articulate, sometimes forceful, and can think on their feet. Second, there are impact and concern; Who is hit by this decision? Who might this decision hurt? These factors are often ignored when voting. Third, the minority has ultimate control of the result. When at odds with voting's outcome, all they must do is nothing. Or worse. The infamous capitol riot of January 2021 proves this point. A 51% majority may carry the day, but implementing tight voting becomes a callous activity with more than its share of gripes.

After voting to keep their creative activities the same as the prior semester (reading, writing and journaling in 15-minute segments), teacher Kevin Hoonan (1996: p. 28) garnered disruption from two middle school boys. After reversing his field and collaborating, the outcome was for students to set their own priorities during the hour. Moreover, his students decided the former division of labor was not even worth considering. This overturned their ballot! Only moments before, repeating the earlier course of action was the outcome of their vote.

Setting Leaders Free

Blending impact and concern into leading is a straightforward task for those who spell out their values. Where competing theories require leaders to change – consider Stephen Covey's Seven Habits of Highly Effective People and Colin Powell's 13 Rules of Leadership -- the Bi-Polar model invites them to become more authentic. Positioning oneself along the chart begins the moment leaders examine their values. Bi-Polar leadership neither clarifies values nor raises skills. Rather, it provides a framework, a home for those tools. The result is color, vitality, flexibility, and a proactive dynamic – overseers choosing interventions, not feeling pushed and pulled by events. To reiterate, *managing* participatory management lets leaders become more of themselves, not less. Dr. Jon Kabat Zinn, founder of the stress reduction clinic at the University of Massachusetts, writes, "It is impossible to become like somebody else. (To reduce stress) your only hope is to become more fully yourself" (Kabat Zinn, 1990, p. 36).

Rewards

Twin-poled leadership has rewards that go beyond internal harmony and personal growth. With the model in place, leaders increase ownership in solutions, ease implementation, lift self-esteem, nourish other esteem, raise productivity, and disarm departmental competition. With Bi-Polar leading, employers revitalize their workforce. Such flexible leading promises to energize the factory floor, stimulate creative thinking, and ready workers to take ownership when implementing solutions. Coaxing, coaching, correcting, and disciplining are all left to a minimum.

MEASURING TOOLS FOR BI-POLAR LEADING

Flexible leading corresponds to an indicator, as does the Hersey/ Blanchard design. But for leaders locating themselves on the Hersey/ Blanchard curve, this means using descriptors internal to the group. This confines H/B leaders to authority, even if authority varies by degree. Twin-poled leaders, on the other hand, add external measures. Such measures can then be ranked according to individual preference. This gives leaders a personalized values system, a lens through which to view their selection of styles. The resulting overlay then applies to choosing methods, not solutions. For solution finding, the values of the group come into play -- unless, of course, the leader chooses authority. In that case, the leader's values have control throughout, meaning of the process and of the solution as well. Below, the left column ranks my values when I began The Collaborative Center in 1989. Thirty years of tinkering has meant personal growth and change, (a point about which my friends sometimes agree). Today, employees and my students are more likely to know me by the schedule on the right. Although as a reader, you may wonder why I chose these values, or ranked them as I did, that type of exercise is irrelevant. Subordinates don't need to know your reasoning. They need to see what you believe and to observe you being consistent to your beliefs, especially as you shift among styles. Your standards and your consistency will become clear. They mark you as their leader.

The Author-as-Leader

VALUES (1989)   VALUES (Today)

Policy   Safety   High

Safety   Impact

Time (Available)	Concern	
Control (my need for)	Trust	
		W
Knowledge	Flexibility	
		E
Trust	Knowledge	
		I
Closeness	Closeness	
		G
Impact	Mood	
		H
Concern	Priorities	
		T
Mood (mine)	Policy	
Priorities	Time	
Flexibility	Control	
		Low

(Source: The Author)

Think about what is important to you as you position yourself along the chart. For example, if you generally want accountability, you probably lean to the left. If you prefer participation, you tend toward the right. The job of teasing these abstract terms into detailed descriptors falls to each leader. Look under the surface of the words. Does "involvement" mean connecting, bonding, fresh ideas, sharing energy, engagement, a sounding board? When you can list what you believe are the benefits of involvement, you will be looking in the direction of your values.

Summary and Conclusion

Corralling Millennials, hitching them to the company wagon, and moving forward with energy and pace is a task unlike challenges faced by employers of the Industrial Era. The command hierarchy once identified exactly who was in charge and who was accountable to whom. But today, "Boss management fails because it limits both the quality of the work and the production of the worker. Its use actually causes most of the problems we are trying to prevent" (Glasser, W.) In reality this means leaders who rely on command-and-control are causing problems they are paid to fix. At the same time, leaders who are enamored with raw participation have trouble moving quickly. Setting priorities is put at jeopardy. And participation, crudely defined, lacks an integrated process.

To engage Millennials, some balance between collaboration and top-down leading is required. The Bi-Polar model introduces such a balance. The collaborative process brings a discrete set of steps. The next chapter shows the advantages in selecting a 'base' for leading without sacrificing methods at the opposing end of the Bi-Polar chart.

Chapter 5

Locating Your Leader Base

A Word About the Bi-Polar Chart

First and foremost, my bi-polar chart is mine. It is for me alone. You will be designing your own menu depending on the styles you include and where you place them on your template. I want to show you why I placed the styles as I did in order to help with your design. I put the methods, or intervention styles where I thought it made sense to reach a decision. For styles based in authority, it figured to have the decisive spot at one, far left on the chart. (At the top left, decisions remain with authority, although the phony consultant and phony collaborator go to great lengths to make it appear otherwise.)

Voting illustrates a similar point. The majority needs to be placed just beyond mid-range. Should voting conclude without a majority, there is no decision to be had. This doesn't disguise the fact that the minority holds uncommon control of the outcome. On January 13, 2021, Senator Mitch McConnel voted to acquit former president Trump based on his opinion the House could not impeach, since Mr. Trump was a lame-duck president, having been voted out of office. This followed a *loss in the senate on McConnel's very question*. Such is the influence of minorities.

On the right side of my chart, I have unanimous deciding -- jury trials, lottery, and skills tests. Drawing straws is a lottery that can be used regarding insubstantial matters. Years ago, I worked as a cottage counselor at a juvenile detention center. There, it was not unusual to take our charges -- some of them high-risk offenders – to the basketball court, shooting free throws to decide casual matters, like who gets the extra dessert or who picks the movie for T.V. These approaches add a subtle flavor of participation to an otherwise command-and-control culture.

Readers may disagree with my placement and should feel free to change it to suit themselves. Change is good here because it means you will be adjusting your own creation. No matter what renowned leaders tell you, one size leadership does not fit all. Remember the values which guide you when deciding. They are the final word in making your chart function in your behalf. This works because like the athlete who keeps his eyes on the ball, his subconscious mind will direct his hands to move to meet it.

I'm fond of saying the leader 'drops down' from the neutral spot to a preferred style depending on events. Most of us have three or four preferred styles, ones we know how to implement and are comfortable with. Typically, these include directing, consulting, voting, and delegating. Some have more, perhaps even six or seven favored styles. To energize employees, the more the better so long as the confidence of the leader remains intact. And the neutral position gives leaders ample time for creativity, for sharing feedback and for managing-by-roaming-around.

Having a preferred base is different. Earlier I described collaboration as the *operative* pole on the right side of my chart. For the leader based in collaboration, that pole is the option of first refusal. In other words, everything is negotiable except that which proves non-negotiable. In the 1990s, when so much went wrong with participation, Seattle television's Almost Live did a sketch with the cast attempting to collaborate while smoke drifted in beneath the meeting room door. Point made! Some issues are not negotiable no matter the leader's primary choice.

For leaders based in authority, directing others is the option of first refusal, meaning nothing is negotiable except that which demands participation. Resistance to authority, when it prevails, will dislodge authoritarians from their base. In that event, authoritarians can at least hope skills with a more participatory style will carry them through.

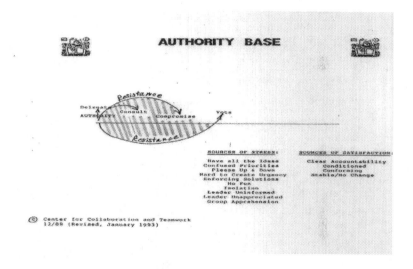

Being removed from power is not the only threat facing leaders based in authority. The following elements are sources of stress.

- They must have all the ideas
- They have difficulty setting priorities
- They feel they must please up and down the chain of command
- If everything is urgent, where is the urgency?
- Difficulty enforcing solutions
- They work in isolation
- They are uninformed and underappreciated

- Their employees are apprehensive
- They are having no fun

Contrast these stressors with authority's sources of satisfaction, Clear accountability, Conditioned response, Conforming demeanor, and Stable environment, No change. Now contrast these elements with stressors and satisfiers under a collaborative culture. First the stressors.

- Time is required to collaborate
- New behavior
- Non-conforming with the past
- Facilitation skills necessary
- Period of adjustment

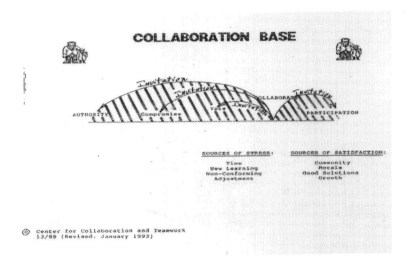

Sources of satisfaction; Sense of community, High morale, Better solutions, Greater creativity, and Personal and Economic growth. These factors more than make up for the time required to decide, which by itself, decreases once collaboration becomes part of the culture.

(Keep in mind, this book is about formal learning, learning

by-the-numbers. Once mastered, practice can be informal, providing added satisfaction. For example, auto repair lease holder Bryan Kelly saw the time was ripe to end his contract and purchase the shop. The property owner asked 1.7 million and Bryan countered with 1.4 million. Rather than deteriorate into a typical real estate deal, both sides express a need to stay close to the appraised value. This they estimated at 1.5. They shook hands and the appraisal came in at 1.55 million.)

Starting at Top Left

The phony collaborator is an unfortunate place to be caught. Your employees would rather you simply use your authority to decide. Anything less will cause yourself and others to lose faith in the collaborative process. Information you need for deciding will gradually dry up. The same is true for the phony consultant. (If you must overrule information which you get by consulting, explain why you do so. This will assure you of your sources and keep deliberations in good faith.)

Manipulations come in two forms – healthy and toxic. At one time in the past, I was in route for an assignment when my trainer said, *"They tell me you're not good enough to carry my briefcase."* Why, I sprang into action like a creepy little toady as we were crossing the street. I doubt someone could get by with that ploy with a Millennial. I remember the stupid feeling that came over me when I realized how unhealthy I was.

Healthy manipulations meet an unspoken need say, to avoid a lengthy conversation. We adults often use manipulation to deal with children. I consider appealing to one's ESI (enlightened self-interest) to be a manipulation of sorts. "If you mow the lawn, you'll have money and can use the car on Saturday night." When President Trump appeared in public atypically wearing a face mask, reporters suggested someone had gotten to his enlightened self-interest.

Delegated authority. Worth remembering here, is you can delegate authority but not accountability. This irony bemused leaders during the last iteration of collaborating, occurring during decentralized decision-making of the 1990s. It is as true as it is realistic today. Today, the leader is thought of as a facilitator, more than a decider. Here is Tom Gordon on the topic: "The leader doesn't solve problems. She sees that problems get solved." Thus, the responsibility remains with the leader and the debate over accountability is a red herring.

Leadership at Bottom Left

Co-Leaders, Lewis and Clark. Despite the military axiom that there must be a solitary chain of command, Lewis and Clark have long set a precedent for duality at the top. The two were also rotating leaders, sharing decisions based on geography (Clark) and biological findings (Lewis). Nevertheless, history records them as co-leaders, and they are my favorite example based on their success with the expedition's men. Settled in temporary quarters at the mouth of the Columbia River, in what must have been a paradise after their harrowing journey, every man chose to return to St. Louis with their benefactors.

Anti-Authoritarian. The chronicles of the Marine Corps record few tales of anti-authoritarian behavior, none as famous as that of Major General O. P. Smith at the Chosin reservoir in the Korean mountains during the winter of 1950. Although badgered by General MacArthur to speed his march to the Yalu, Smith stopped at the Chosin. Smith's intelligence patrols told him they were surrounded by Chinese. Smith was right to defy MacArthur. History records the presence of 20 Communist divisions totaling some 300,000 men. Smith's Division had 15,000 combatants in three awkwardly split regiments. His flanks were open by more than 40 miles.

What followed was the epic retreat in the annals of the Marine

Corps where Smith rendered five of the Communist divisions combat ineffective. "We were just attacking in a new direction." Smith's story can be tracked on Google. Search "The man who saved 15,000 Marines."

Usurped authority. General Smith's is also the story of usurped authority. It is a cautionary tale – for his rebellious behavior, many thought Smith was denied a nomination for the Congressional Medal of Honor. He was later bypassed for Commandant of Marines, the Marine Corps' top job.

Multiple Leaders:

Consulting Leaders. The beginning of teamwork. (No leader has enough solutions by himself)

Enlightened Self Interest. As mentioned, appealing to a worker's ESI can be an effective way to enlist cooperation even outright support. No decision-making process is more important than employees putting their shoulders to the wheel, and the appeal to ESI does the job while leaving collaboration in place as an option.

Mediation. Mediation resembles collaboration in almost every detail. Leaders turn to mediation, either external or internal, when they are concerned with outcomes. They turn to collaboration when they are concerned with building (or maintaining) relationships. Only the objective is different. The process is the same.

Compromise. Another method that concerns itself with relationships is compromise. It can be argued that folks enter a compromise willing to give up half of their goals. Couples often compromise in order to protect a relationship, as in, "My turn to choose where for dinner. Last time you picked." This can be an opportune way to avoid disagreement. It can take on the appearance of rotating authority should couples reciprocate over time. Sadly, with adversarial politics, compromise can be detrimental. Building relationships is seldom in play. In divisive times, when competing operatives see one another as opponents, compromise can be a way to frustrate rivals and force them to surrender their goals. When that happens, the American Public gets little from outcomes and nothing by way of relationships. (See chart below.)

Referral. When leaders feel less than confident in either method or goals, they can refer dispassionately to a higher authority – in legal terms, a court of appeals. Our judicial system is based on referral. When it works, it is a thing of beauty, respected the world over. When it fails, as it did with O.J. Simpson or Steven Avery,* it becomes a farce.

Democratic vote. This book has not been shy about criticizing the limits of democratic voting. Based as it is on adversarial argument, whenever it fails to gain unanimous decisions, its faults are laid bare; it delivers less than can be supported and does nothing in the for relationships. If you doubt the force of minorities, look at Black Lives Matter and its impact over the second half of 2020.

Laissez Faire Leadership. Leadership by default – *not to decide is to decide.*

Straw Voting. A non-binding tabulation that sets the stage for deeper deliberations. Most do not know that in high-profile legal trials, juries take a straw vote before starting their deliberation.

Group defiance. The Garfield teachers' refusal to administer the Measure of Academic Progress exam tells the tale of group defiance (Chapter 6). Professional ballplayers who kneel before games display group defiance.

Collaboration. Democracy's new model. It is the only model for assuring best outcomes, best camaraderie, and best practice at the same time. The chart below shows how collaboration contrasts with

---

* Steven Avery served 18 years in prison on a rape charge when the sheriff had information another man committed the crime. On his exoneration, he sued for 36 million dollars. Months later, he was charged with murder, convicted and sentenced to life. Avery has served thirty years for crimes he possibly didn't commit, alleging the sheriff again fabricated evidence against him. (For more information, google Steven Avery or search Netflix, Making a Murderer)

compromise. Note how in the best-case compromise (B), goals are surrendered by one-half in order that relationships can be maximized. In the worst case (C), little is gained in either goals or relationships. The collaborative area (A) is where both can be maximized.

Razi – I'm not happy with this chart. db

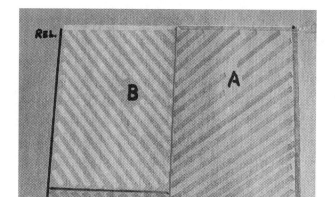

Source: The Author

C = Adversarial compromise. Meeting half needs while sacrificing relationship.

B = Healthy compromise. Sacrificing half needs while enhancing/ protecting relationship.

A = Collaborative Solution, meeting needs and building relationship.

Ratification/Veto. Employers may appeal to workers to ratify a decision already taken. If the approval is denied, this would constitute a veto; a good reason to return to the Bi-Polar chart.

Non-Negotiable Styles

Self-explanatory. The non-negotiable leader deceives himself by thinking that vanquishing his opponents means he is a leader. In effect, he is merely getting his own small way, invariably to the detriment of his organization.

A Study in Bi-Polar Leading

Teachers make myriad decisions every waking moment; some say hundreds per day. Here is one day in the life of Mary Banister, fifth grade teacher at a nearby parochial school. Mary's entertaining report is an example due to its volume of problem-solving as well as its flexibility. Here is Mary's report.

"When I arrived at school, there were no major decisions awaiting me. Once class began, things moved rapidly across my bi-polar index. I was the <u>authoritarian</u> as the students entered the room and I assigned the usual morning tasks. As we read the social studies text for the day, I moved to <u>rotating authority</u>, letting students take turns leading the discussion. I quickly became a <u>mediator</u> in the case of one student putting down another in a note-passing incident. I bopped back to <u>authoritarian</u> as one student in a moment of blind stupidity attempted to cut himself with some scissors. (Blood work would have to wait at least until science class!). During the cooperative learning session, I <u>compromised</u> with a student in the way part of the assignment could be required. Next, I made a <u>referral</u> of a student to another student for help with a problem. When we had to select a classroom representative to read a petition for Mass the following day, I let the students <u>vote</u> on their own representative. Our principal thought this was too liberal a move, but the students handled it well.

"I appealed to the students' <u>Enlightened Self-Interest</u> to create quiet in the halls since we had to pass the principal's office on our way to the lunchroom. During our science experiment, I moved to a <u>consultative</u>

position as I believe that self-discovery is this area makes for more powerful learning. While reading and responding to the student's daily journals, I <u>defaulted</u> (?). A student wanted me to make another student do something to her specifications and I said that she would have to talk to that student and work it out herself. I didn't feel that this was a <u>delegated authority</u> as I felt it was never my decision in the first place.

"At our afternoon staff meeting, my department had a chance to review our playground rotations on the *Big Toy* (inflatable) and by <u>unanimous</u> decision and much discussion, we let the schedule remain as is. On the topic of parent-teacher conferences we made a <u>referral</u> as a department to the principal. Feeling we were on a roll, we <u>unanimously</u> agreed to check into a new curriculum on gang intervention for our school.

The next decision was an act of <u>group defiance</u>. We were to have a scheduled assembly which we felt was unsuitable to our students for a variety of reasons and we all decided we were unwilling to have our classes attend. We'll have to see if a mandate to attend comes down from higher authority. (Sometimes the power is there only if we make the right decision.) Another <u>referral</u> was made to the central administration regarding our Archdiocesan in-service day for Fall. (Soon after, our department <u>unanimously</u> agreed to leave the meeting as we had other things to attend to before we could leave for the day.) "I went home long enough to hold a sick daughter for ten minutes, check in on another daughter's homework, stop to see if my husband still recognized me and stir the crock pot. Then I ran out to my next meeting.

"I was hoping to see some <u>collaborative decision-making</u> at the site-based management council. Parents interested in applying for our few seats on the council were to attend. What happened was a <u>delegated authority</u> – the principal told (us) parents that we could have 3 (of 14) seats on the council but <u>compromised</u> with us to make an extra seat available for the PTA president. I think she was shocked that the few parents who did come to the meeting were so vocal and adamant that we were not satisfied with what was being presented to us. We were able to get our needs on the table. Those were,

To have equal numbers of parents on the council as teachers.

To allow all interested parents to attend the district trainings

To have meeting times which were convenient to parents' hours and not be limited to hours in the teachers' day.

"(We) parents were determined not to be railroaded into accepting a less than adequate proposition. The principal requested a meeting where the district could present their needs for council make-up and meeting times. This process promised to be <u>collaborative</u>. Most of us came away from the meeting with a mixture of commitment and hope.

"Next, I had 5 minutes to caucus and <u>vote</u> with the voter registrars. The result was the return of the Election Day Bake Sale, one of those fuzzy moments that turn elections into favorable outcomes for bond issues. (Call this manipulation; I think of it as mutual backscratching.)

"Next was the PTA Executive committee meeting. First on our agenda was our treasurer's report. We made more money than anticipated and faced a decision on whether to purchase insurance in case someone ran off with our funds. This was a <u>default</u> decision as I was the only concerned parent. We then <u>compromised</u> on a choice to pay for an assembly which was at first proposed as being free. Then hidden costs appeared. The school budget will split the costs with the PTA.

"I was a <u>consultant</u> as I explained to the committee that a monetary grant I had applied for in connection with our new Homework Night program to begin next month. Our principal offered to <u>mediate</u> with the librarian and myself for use of computers during these events. I suggested we <u>collaborate</u> between us, and we resolved the issue favorably for both.

"The next issue was designing our new school sweatshirts, moving away from our traditional colors, which also happen to be gang related. The decision was cooperative and <u>unanimous</u> among those present, but it was only a <u>straw vote</u> – We had to proceed without a quorum in order to have the shirts available for holiday ordering. If we can't <u>ratify</u> the motion in arrears and the others don't like them, they don't have to buy them! Should be no problem.

"The meeting progressed around the room in a <u>rotating authority</u> manner as each person brought the rest up to speed on committee work and current issues. We all <u>unanimously</u> declined the position of Levy Chair, knowing how much work it entailed. After the principal left, we agreed on our views of <u>group defiance</u> regarding the current proposal for site-based management. It took some <u>negotiating</u>, but I think we talked our hothead into a calmer approach. Our principal continues to listen. And hover. We don't know if she will be a <u>collaborator</u> or an <u>arbitrator</u>. Must wait and see."

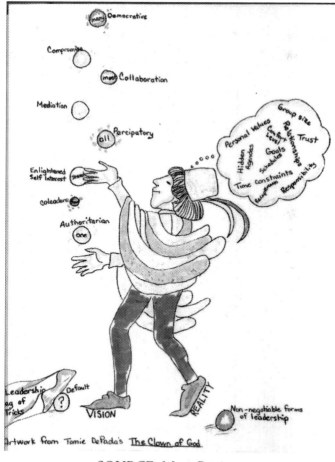

SOURCE: Mary Banister

Summary

Mary's report displays a nimble mind, a flexible spirit, and a capacity for taking charge of her chart, *not her students*. She keeps her options open, and she is firmly aware of them all. This way, rather than let herself be pushed and pulled by events, she directs activities without directing the people involved. In terms of *personal* power, * this is a compelling position to hold.

Such is the life of the bi-polar leader. Collaborative decisions can be infrequent, but nevertheless inviting to constituents, as children prove by their fascination with Mary's multi-faceted approach. I am asked, "How often should I collaborate?" My answer is the same — follow your instincts, *and those of your employees*. If pressed, I might suggest once-a-week for starters. Your situation is alive with possibility. How soon do you want to change the culture in your workplace? The call is entirely up to you.

ON POWER: "*Power is the capacity to experience yourself fully, coupled with an effective response to that experience — the capacity to know who you are and to take action in the world that represents that inner experience.*"

John Thomas Wood
The Little Blue Book on Power

Chapter 6

The Making of a Millennial-
No Child Left Behind

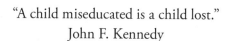

"A child miseducated is a child lost."
John F. Kennedy

According to PEW demographics, millennials are now the dominant group in the workplace. This chapter is a look at their education and No Child Left Behind, the legislation that drives them. The impact of millennial's schooling cannot be understated. Instigated on President George Bush's watch and founded on Texas' unproven model, No Child Left Behind was designed to equalize education over districts, schools, and classrooms, and to lift academic performance on an international scale. Its goals were never achieved, neither nationally nor in comparison with districts around the globe. As an unintended consequence, only the military gained in the exchange. Battling through thirty years of war in the Middle East, the Army's all-volunteer units were suddenly aided by their finest recruits – the result of some youngsters' failure adjust to classroom anxieties.

In hindsight, the thirteen-year thrust toward standardizing tests is today looked upon as a major error. In minority and low-income districts where children were not competing, dropout rates soared. By 2011, individual states, realizing the high cost of testing, were waiving and even reversing the requirements of No Child Left Behind (NCLB). State after state demanded relief from its draconian demands. In Maryland, Montgomery County School Superintendent Joshua Starr spurned NCLB Funding, citing his district's own nationally recognized evaluation system. He called for a three-year moratorium on standardized tests. (Strauss, 2012). Idaho, Montana and South Dakota threatened to ignore the law altogether (McNeil, 2011). Testifying before congress, New York City teacher Jia Lee called NCLB a "great crime" (Lee, 2015). In an interview, Seattle Education Association President Jonathan Knapp told me, "Almost everything about No Child Left Behind is wrong" (Personal conversation, November 5, 2014). It was not the tests as such that disturbed kids. Teens say the tests were challenging; they were a rush. It was the myopic focus on preparation that troubled teachers and children alike. In the classroom, the pressure on teacher and child was intense. Berkeley professor David Kirp called schools a 'pressure cooker' and wrote, "students have become test-taking robots, sitting through as many as 20 standardized tests a year" (Kirp, 2015, para 5). Everyone -- teachers, parents, administrators, citizens, students -- wants children to be evaluated. But we want them to grow emotionally and socially as well, perhaps equally during their hours in school. In the 1960s Abraham Maslow decried "education which concerned itself with grades, credits and diplomas rather than wisdom, understanding and good judgment" (Hoffman, E., 1988, p. 104).

More recently, educator Mary Futrell wrote, "The standards movement and the requirements of No Child Left Behind made it abundantly clear: we can't simply set goals and then punish people for not achieving them." (Rubin, H., 2009, p. xi) As an increasing number of parents opt their children out of standardized tests, they do so for many reasons, "including the stress they believe it brings on young students, discomfort with tests being used to gauge teacher performance, fear that corporate influence is overriding education, and concern that test prep is narrowing curricula down to the minimum needed to pass an exam" (Zezima, 2013, para. 2). Merrimack College Dean of Education, Dan Butin adds, ". . . assessments can never tell the full story of a child" (Butin, D., 2012).

In 2015, Congress faced an uproar created by its own law. Kentucky Senator Rand Paul (R) "wants to repeal the law and says many students have been failed by the current system" (n/a, Town News Online, January 29, 2015). Senator Patty Murray, the ranking Democrat on the Senate's Education Committee, wrote, "NCLB has proved to be a deeply broken law with unrealistic requirements. It is hindering [teachers'] efforts and needs to be fixed" (Murray, 2015).

WHAT'S REALLY AT STAKE WITH HIGH STAKES TESTS?

Beyond frustrated students, here is the problem. The push toward standardized tests is more than a way to measure individual progress. It is also a way to hand out pass/fail grades to schools, thereby holding teachers accountable, but in only a single dimension, content. As former National Superintendent of the Year, Heath Morrison asked, "Why are we in a rush to do all this testing, then use it for accountability for schools and for accountability for teachers?"

This quickly became a political issue. Morrison called testing "an egregious waste of taxpayer dollars that won't help kids" (The Charlotte Observer, Dec. 27, 2012, para. 12). So long as emotional and social growth are excluded from the equation, three things are wrong with the NCLB approach. First, the grades handed to schools are a false litmus test for progress; damage is not being measured.

While in cross-section, the 2015 drop-out rate shows signs of recovery, the United States high school graduation rate ranks in the bottom fourth of developed nations (OECD, 2019). This is because in low-income communities – home to so-called drop-out factories -- less than half the freshman class would graduate on time. (Koebler, 2011, para 1). Children from these locales were the poor and minority children George Bush's education law was designed to assist (Hefling, 2015). Yet more than eight thousand students were leaving formal schooling daily, most from impoverished communities (StatisticBrain.org, 2014). So much for No Child Left Behind. Education had triggered waves of youth left behind like the Tune In, Turn On, Drop Out druggie generation of the 1960s. Impoverished youngsters were voting with their feet. They are leaving with a jaundiced view of adults in general and officialdom in particular.

Second, education proceeds not just in math and reading, but also in breadth and depth, such as art, music, theater, interpersonal communications. In the early days of the Bush administration, Washington State's Commission on Student Learning met to hammer out standards for No Child Left Behind. I attended those meetings as an observer. Although members included district superintendents, most commissioners came from Corporate America.

Fredrick Taylor, the father of time-and-motion studies – Taylor introduced such force-feeding to industrial production in 1881 – could not have been more pleased. Taylor's effort was to standardize the nation's workforce by timing factory workers on their every move. Although scientific management (Taylorism) as a distinct theory was obsolete by the 1930s, most of its themes are subliminal parts of industrial management today (ibiblio.org., 2013, para. 2). The problem is teachers are not industrialists. They want teaching to be about creativity, civics, and character development. They know and understand the in-depth growing that must take place in their charges. They are the professionals. They can be trusted to know schooling's larger purpose whereas corporate executives cannot.

Frederick Taylor is simply another hawk for content. As educator/ author Dr. Hank Rubin wrote, "Despite the fact that today, most schools continue to prepare young learners to be storage banks of knowledge and skills that they can summon on demand and exhibit on high stakes tests, we know that this type of accountability captures only a small portion of what we need from public education – and what tomorrow's learners will need to succeed." (Rubin, H., 2009, p. 26). Teacher and author Jesse Hagopian adds, "I'm opposed to these tests because they narrow what education is supposed to be about and they lower kids' horizons. I think collaboration, imagination, critical thinking skills are all left off these tests and can't be assessed by circling in A, B, C, or D" (Zezima, 2013, para. 6).

Finally, there is the military axiom that leaders dare not issue directives that cannot be enforced. The loss of influence and respect are simply too great. At Seattle's Garfield High School, January 9, 2013, was examination day. No kids showed up to be tested. In fact, no tests were given. Garfield teachers boycotted the exam, refusing to administer it. Saying the MAP test (Measure of Academic Progress) was flawed and students were sabotaging the outcomes because they knew the results made no difference in their grade, Garfield's staff unanimously defied their district. There is no greater disrespect for leadership than to flout the leader's dictates. And there is no greater trepidation on the part of leaders than a mandate of their own would reap an act of mutiny.

Parents have also taken up the cudgel, willingly joining the acrimony over accountability. In Compton, California, hundreds of protesters marched on the Los Angeles education headquarters demanding a charter takeover of their neighborhood school. The

Parent Revolution, which championed the McKinley School march under California's Parent Empowerment Act of 2010, heralded the action as if the French had again stormed the Bastille. The group called December 8, 2010, an historic day (McDonald, 2010). True, some 200 schools (of 800) in the Los Angeles District had failed to meet No Child Left Behind standards (Op/Ed Seattle Times online, Dec. 28, 2012), and as Parent Revolution chief Benjamin Austin says, apart from his revolution, "There is no consequence for failure and no reward for success" (Austin, 2012). So, Austin would add another layer to the demand for accountability. In a demonstration of futility, California's so-called trigger law, which granted take-over power to parents, was watered "almost beyond recognition" by Julia Brownley, the state's Education Committee chairwoman (Austin, 2009). This weakening of the trigger law took place after Brownley entertained dozens of parents testifying about the importance of parent influence in their local schools. Brownley's version of the new law meant failing schools would foster nothing more than a "meaningless and patronizing hearing" (Austin, 2009). The chairwoman announced her version with "great fanfare, saying she had heard the call of the parents" (Austin, 2009). In fact, Brownley flinched. She placed herself as a phony consulter, that high-risk position, top left on the twin polar chart. Outraged by Brownley's stance, McKinley's parents marched.

Arguably, a charter operator for McKinley Elementary might have succeeded. (The issue became moot; a legal technicality caused the parent's appeal to be thrown out). However, the outcome is not what matters here. It is the way things get decided that puts McKinley children at risk. Reports of retribution, threats, and even physical violence punctuated the divide. (Wilson, 2011, pg.1) Even the name *revolution* seemed overpowering. Inflamed rhetoric does nothing to further a good-faith caucus between educators, parents, the larger community, and certainly students themselves. The McKinley charter petition proved to be a nonstarter. But to carry on the debate in hurtful terms set a dangerous precedent for

McKinley's kids. They will learn about political power soon enough. They will need a more creative solution while they are still innocent and can profit from a collegial approach. Here, again is Dr. Rubin; "The message of my book, *COLLABORATIVE LEADERSHIP*, is families, communities, educators, business leaders and policy makers are engaged in an ongoing relationship and share responsibility for the education of our children and youth. This teamwork . . . deserves much more attention if we want to improve our schools and other public agencies to insure our children's future" (Rubin, 2009, p. 42).

NEW STANDARDS FOR A NEW AGE

Rubin's ongoing relationship means parties would have to abandon the Industrial anthem in which competition, not cooperation guides the debate. Today neither Generation Z nor Generation Alpha are growing up in the Industrial Age. They were not even born in it. A list of desired characteristics of workers during the Industrial Age comes from Irving Burstiner. It was published near the end of that era, in 1984. In his classic, but dated lament, Burstiner called for a revival of the values shown below. • Good level of productivity • Consistency • Honesty • Loyalty to the firm • No rocking the boat • Pleasant personality • Promptness • Proper behavior on the job • Regular attendance and • Respect for authority

What if attributes of today's worker could connect with Burstiner's tenets while simultaneously replacing those values? For each of the 1984 bullets, a behavior characteristic of the Age of Information can be substituted. Keep in mind that today, no one person has enough information to pronounce decisions in solitude, even in consultation -- which too, can smack of isolation. For good level of productivity, one can name good level of creativity. For consistency, contribution; for honesty, full disclosure; for loyalty to the firm, loyalty to the process; for pleasant personality, effective personality; for no rocking the boat, rocking the boat; for promptness, results;

for proper behavior, innovative behavior; for respect for authority, respect for ideas; and for regular attendance, total attendance. Whatever Burstiner's intention, his qualities no longer fit today's workplace. In fact, so long as content and accountability remain pivotal to school reform, corporate philanthropies such as the Gates and Broad Foundations will aggregate power, districts will continue to circle the wagons, young people will continue to drop out, parents will continue to receive carefully vetted information, teachers will continue their frustration and principals will continue to hold tight to the reins. No one can fault the administrator who says, "*If my ship is going down, I will be the one at the helm.*" Yet together, these factors stifle collaboration, create winners and losers, and perpetuate the competitive mentality of an outmoded age.

THE PHENOMENON OF BELONGING

If one word could summarize the difference between the Industrial Age and the Age of Information, that word would be *belonging*. As it stands today, education is a closed community. It is closed to parents and it is closed to children. There is significant debate whether it exists for children at all. Austin's League of Education Voters believes it exists for adults. Michelle Rhee, the ousted chancellor of District of Columbia schools, echoes the league's position. Rhee states, "Policy makers, district administrators, and school boards. . . have created a bureaucracy that is focused on the adults instead of students" (Rhee, 2010, p. 41). Except for an occasional supporting role, belonging to the school community is rarely an option for children and families.

In one small Caribbean country, airport arrivals are greeted with two large signs: BELONGERS and VISITORS. As Pew Foundation Director Suzanne Morse writes, "The volumes written today about leadership fail to recognize the motivation and the necessity of belonging in leadership preparation and selection. The heart of leadership, belonging to a community and its common interest is lost. All learning. . . is rooted in the human need to feel a sense of belonging and contributing to a community" Morse, S. (2009), p.17).

In our transitioning culture, there is evidence that children are positioned for belonging more than is commonly known. Why are they being denied? Once again, Maslow's hierarchy is revealing. Maslow distinguished between basic needs and what he called Meta, or growth needs. In cross section, basic needs have been provided through the prosperity of the Industrial Era. Still for students to grow socially and emotionally, they must feel they belong. Among the Meta needs that normally are met prior to belonging, Maslow included self-esteem. (Anyone who thinks children's esteem is not vital to a school culture should try mocking a child in the classroom. Action from the ACLU will not be far behind!) For four decades, the theme of self-esteem has been pivotal to the school curriculum, creating a disconnect concerning whether or not to incorporate youthful voices in decision-making. Children are prepared to assume a huge sense of belonging. In fact, they go to great lengths to belong – they simply do not include adults in their community. (See Maslow's Needs, p. 9) In a collaborative environment, belonging becomes a reality. You cannot avoid it.

In Coeur d'Alene, Idaho, teacher Melita Clary collaborated with her sixth graders over semester rules. "Actually, I didn't need to give anything beyond my need for order," she writes. "If any idea went against my need, the rest of the children spoke out against it." For Clary's new students, cooperation was not the norm. Clary's class came with a reputation for trouble. After they collaborated, one girl came to her in tears, "You're the first teacher that gave our class a chance."

Teachers collaborating with students, parents collaborating with teachers -- parents will not march in protest on a collaborative school; their children will not allow it. In fact, it is children who will remind us to collaborate. Psychologist/author Charlotte Kasl describes a stalemate when her 14-year-old daughter wanted to see a movie and mother was too sick to drive her. After examining needs, they reached a solution together—a neighboring friend would drive, and the two girls could spend an overnight together. When Kasl next faced a row with her daughter, the youngster pleaded, "Can it be like the time at the movies? Tell me the two sides" (Kasl, C., 1989, p. 271). Clary, too, sometimes overlooks the chance to collaborate. She writes, "You can be sure my kids will remind me."

Leader Effectiveness promoter Tom Gordon's own children have been known to force the issue. Once when Gordon was about to pronounce a decision, his daughter held up an index finger and mouthed, Method One, the win-lose method described in chapter two. Gordon quickly backtracked and asked for his daughter's needs. Junior high school teacher Gloria Tyler says, "When students partner with their teacher and are allowed to join in the decision-making process, they begin to 'own' part of the classroom system. In that ownership, they become less disruptive, instead more relaxed and engaged learners" (Tyler, 2017, personal communication).

THE INADEQUACY OF AUTHORITY

Why would business leaders not welcome alternatives to authority? Look at the factors that are leveraging here; first, just as in education, the corporate world is dramatically linked. No single person has all the answers. Bosses that rely exclusively on the hierarchy of their position are routinely referred to as Type A or micro managers. To avoid a stigma, they hold meetings. Meetings that disregard the voices of subordinates lose the feedback leaders need. Meetings that take place simply to announce a decision are a disaster. This is no more so than when the convener has positioned herself as having heard their workers' concerns. As California's Julia Brownley learned, those only result in hostility and resentment. Children need to prepare for a highly interconnected world. They need leaders who can listen and can spark creativity; when it comes to decision-making, they need a genuine airing of ideas. And why not? Renowned industrial psychologist Rensis Likert has observed, when managers allow participation, those at the top actually have more influence rather than less. "That is, in a team environment, the more power you give to someone else, the more you have for yourself" (Goble, 2005, p. 20).

Second, there is the business of social media. Most of our young people use Facebook and texting to exchange ideas with contemporaries across the country and even globe. The phenomenon has been the topic of study, and its bonding element among young people cannot be denied. Millennials are simply accustomed to connecting, uniting on a genuinely intimate level. They need the same from their workplace. We should not overlook that in many cases, they get their intimacy, their togetherness from social media. The tipping point remains distant before the younger generations enjoy similar fruits from workplace collaborations.

Third, the Industrial Hierarchy has collapsed. Apart from military and para-military organizations, command-and-control has done nothing to redeem itself since Harvard's Rosabeth Moss Kanter wrote that the hierarchy would collapse of its own weight. Kanter likened global economic competition to the Olympics. The winners in these games would be nonhierarchical, co-operative, focused on process—the way things are done. They would also, she said, have a dose of humility. (Kanter, 1989). The flattening of the hierarchy that took place in the '90s was designed to create a more streamlined organization. It did that. But it also riffed mid-level managers and doubled the workload of those who stayed behind. Today, there are even books about Bottom-Up Leadership, for example, How to Manage Your Manager, and Followership: How Followers Are Creating Change and Changing Leaders. Understandably, Top-Down management has lost much of its fabled panache.

Fourth, there is the Bart Simpson Effect – our kids believe they can say anything that comes to mind. Thanks to many years of applied psychology in our nation's schools, children have become remarkably in touch with their inner musings -- and eager to let everyone know what those are. The result is young men and women who are more than outspoken; they believe their every notion must be aired. No wonder they clamor for collaboration after being denied it for so long. Fifth is the business of self-esteem. Unlike most adults, kids were not raised in a culture of sin, guilt and redemption (Leins, C., 2015). They do not comprehend it. Their esteem will not allow. A function of applied psychology that has informed teaching for the past forty years, the esteem movement will never reverse itself. It is here to impact us, well, forever. What that means is children not only gushing with ideas, but also seeing their ideas as necessary to the outcome of an event.

Finally, there is the Information Age, what Warren Bennis calls the Age of Knowledge. (According to Bennis, power in the knowledge economy resides with information workers not with owners or managers, *The Leadership Advantage*, April, 2006). By all measure, The Age of Industry has passed, leaving a legacy of triumph and domination that is being eroded by a global economy, one that sees goods produced abroad. The U.S. economy, on the other hand, is based on service, service that involves the sharing of information. This may seem trite; most know about this shift already. Still, it is a factor because today's young workers know nothing of the heyday of industrial life. They know little of The Greatest Generation, and of the exponential growth that marked the economic wave following World War Two. They only know about their laptops, their tablets, their iPhones, and the information found there, all of which is shared. However we misunderstand Millennials, connecting among others is their world.

Taken together, corporate connectivity, social networking, the demise of the hierarchy, children's verbosity, the self-esteem movement, and the reality of the Information Age all point to collaboration as the way out of the workplace abyss. While the above items might seem enigmatic, a problem to some, they can also be looked at as the ingredients for a collaborative culture. Yes, taken separately they might seem difficult. Taken together, they might simply describe the detritus of the Industrial Era, and the Top-Down model which it brought to bear.

GIVING COLLABORATION A CHANCE

Today we are at a crossroads. The Human Potential Movement of the 1990's failed. It failed because of resistance to viewing the human as our greatest underdeveloped strength. The human being remains an untapped asset. But what does that mean in the face of how leaders lead? It means little more than an invitation, a plea for a second chance. Collaborative endeavor stands like the proverbial low-hanging fruit. The main ingredients are already present – the attending skills of employers and the exuberance of young people – and the cost is nothing save a few minutes away from preconceived agenda. All that is needed is support from the Board Room. . . and patience on the part of the Corporate Agenda.

SUMMARY

Our world's economy and its cast of characters has changed. Once teachers were the workers, principals the managers, children the raw material (and eventual product), and the consumer was business and industry. In today's world, the division of labor is far more complex. Children and teachers together are the workers. Curriculum, books and experience are the raw materials. Creativity and ideas are the product, and the consumer is an entire society. Most important, education's investors were formerly Wall Street and society at large. Now students do the investing. And many of today's youth are withdrawing their equity. Rather than face a classroom where they feel overpowered, they are opting for low paying jobs and the tedious task of living at home. They are simply not willing to be judged on their ability to stockpile knowledge and vomit it up on high-stakes tests. If that's all education is about, some are even willing to risk a future life on the streets. Whether in the classroom or at work, leaders make scores of decisions every day, striving to solve problems that occupy part of each day's labor. Millennials are prepared to take part in those outcomes, at least on occasion and to an extent. They are being blocked leaders' left-over interest in accountability and command-and-control. Collaborative leadership offers a path that employers can follow to bring out the healthy values of today's workers, can give them a sense of belonging to something greater than themselves. It can provide the bonding that keeps children enthusiastic, keeps them learning, and prepares them for a future in an interconnected workplace.

FOOTNOTE: In December, 2015, Congress under its Every Student Succeeds Act, revoked No Child Left Behind. Oversight was returned to the states.

Chapter 7

On Politics, Government and Community

~

*"For the next 18 months, our job is to do
everything we can to create chaos."*
GOP Representative Chip Roy, (Texas) 2021

Introduction:

Our world has never been more in need of collaborative solutions.
Look at what's happening around us. Some misbehavior is by clients
that have fought wars with us and stood to gain Western behavioral
practices to their advantage. Two examples are Iraq and Japan.
On Wednesday, April 13, 2016, the Iraqi Parliament dissolved
into a fistfight. Lawmakers shoved, pushed and threw punches.
Kurdish members of parliament said they arrived to learn that other
lawmakers had broken their name plates. Never much good at it, in
a country that has lived by the sword, Democracy is in danger of
dying by the sword.

In September 2018, there occurred the latest outburst in

the Japanese Legislature, where a string of fistfights punctuated parliamentary actions over the previous 4 years. The 2018 brawl involved dozens, lasted almost 2 minutes and erupted over whether Japan should vote to send troops outside their country, prohibited since WW II. Uganda, Georgia, India, Nepal, and Turkey have all been tarnished by lawmaker fisticuffs in the past two years.

At home in 2021, America was struggling through losses of extraordinary magnitude, giving birth to street-venting of an order not seen since the civil rights days of the 60s. Forty million were unemployed. Quarantine has left us bereft of social contact. Nearly one million deaths from Covid-19 brought us closer to that milestone and the death of George Floyd at the hands Minneapolis police has left a nation anxious and toting a short fuse. When it was lit, as it was in the January 6th insurrection, all measure of civil discourse melted save an equally violent restoring order to the streets. People are not happy any longer simply to cast a vote. Democracy as we know it is at risk.

Chris Wallace the Fox News Sunday host said, "We have to talk not only about what is going on with riots in the street, we have to talk about what is going on among people at the highest levels of our society" (Wallace, 2020). A case in point? In this fractured moment of unrest, President Trump threw a rhetorical match into the flames. "When the looting starts, the shooting starts," he declared in a late-night tweet. (When Billy the Kid became the fastest pistol in the west, gunslingers from all over the place showed up to test his mettle. It seems almost human nature to respond viscerally to provocations like Trump's.) "The episode encapsulated Trump's approach to the presidency and to this time of national crisis, which has upended nearly every aspect of American life" (Pace, 2020).

"The nation is on fire, and the president of the United States is standing there with gasoline," said Rep. Val Demings of Florida (Demings, 2020). "I had hoped that at least for this one time, some of the president's advisers would get to him and try to convince him to be consoler-in-chief," said Rep. Emanuel Cleaver, a Democrat from Missouri. "President Trump was not built for times like this" (Cleaver, 2020).

President Trump condemned the civil rallies in the name of George Floyd. In doing so, he threatened to call out the U.S. Army to patrol the nation's streets and called protesters "radical left-wing agitators." He used the same warning describing his supporters who launched the uprising in D.C. Such attacks across party lines are common to the former president, as is his demagoguery when under duress. Go back to the Bi-Polar chart on page 57. Note the non-negotiable leadership styles. President Trump has governed his entire life by these misguided tenets. Now, even as a defeated president, he presumes to govern his remaining followers by them as he promises a return in 2024.

The institutional weight of representative government is overwhelming. The congress is no better than the commander-in-chief. There is openness only when representatives decide there is openness. Deals are brokered behind closed doors. Debate is often filled with acrimony and speakers lambast their opponents under the pretense of "The gentleman from (fill in the state)." Any longer, there is no 'loyal opposition,' only enemies growling at the gates. In the present situation, the Right accuses Democrats of leading an Anti-Fascist revolution. It even attacks fellow Republicans like Colin Powell and James Mattis for acting like "little Democrats." From the Left, Nancy Pelosi cries, "The enemy is within the House of Representatives!" And where is John McCain, who at least could work both sides of the aisle.

Participatory Democracy; The Missing Link

More than one individual is absent here. It is participatory government that is lacking. John Dewey devoted his life, and philosophical writing toward it. He knew it would be a hard sell. "The path of least trouble is a mental rut already made. It requires troublesome work to undertake the alteration of old beliefs" (Dewey, 1902). "Our representative democracy is not working because the Congress that is supposed to represent the voters does not respond to their needs. I believe the chief reason for this is that it is ruled by a small group of old men" (Chisholm, August 23, 2018).

Shirley Chisholm makes a valid, but superficial point. The issue is complicated. The question cuts deeper than age, gender, and race. I believe congressmen/women have never been taught about participative government. Their legal preparation was about confrontational paths to power. They have not been taught to ask for needs and they hesitate to reveal their own. I would be shocked if one of them came right out and said, "I need to get reelected." Even so, what lies beneath that revelation for each elected official remains personal and patently out of play. In addition, people in power are reluctant to abandon power, to leave power behind. That they as leaders, would be essential in a facilitative role – or that they would gain power by doing so – is beyond their understanding. They are in John Dewey's rut.

A Sense of Citizenship

Citizens are asking for creative ways to encounter problems and issue legislation. They would like to have problem-solving opportunities that "go beyond the polarization of exclusive partisan positions. . . Most of all, they want a sense of community—that all of us are in this together. They want to tackle difficult problems not in anarchic or antagonistic ways but in ways that reflect a new kind of democracy and a sense of citizenship" (Chrislip and Larson, p. 4).

In a collaborative world, differences in power and authority are ignored. "This kind of leadership is characterized by its focus on safeguarding a process rather than on individual leaders taking decisive action." (Ibid, p. 125). Its purpose is, "to discover new approaches for engaging on public issues that break gridlock and heal the divisions of the community" (Ibid, p. 125). The results of effective collaborative leadership are that both sides, leaders and followers get their needs met. The whole person brings himself/ herself to the negotiation, and together as peers, they work to a successful conclusion. In fact, one presumes that a problem occurs primarily when either the leader or an employee is not getting needs addressed. (This is problem with a little 'p.' Problem with a big 'P' is how to pull off the result – How can we meet the needs of employer A at the same time we meet the needs of employee B? How do we care for the needs of official A while we care for the needs of citizen B?)

Leadership: A New Vision

Collaborative leaders are visionary. But not about solutions. They envision how people can work together. They do not call a meeting to pontificate their idea (and gather 'feedback') but take the feedback first. Before Washington State's governor Jay Inslee began studying his Covid-19 plans for reentering the state's economy, he called a press conference and asked for citizens' thoughts – "What are you already doing to stave off the virus?" Only later did he publish his reopening schedule, (revised after the Omicron variant descended upon us). When such leaders engage people constructively and model the new approach, people are empowered; citizens, and leaders get their needs met. A deeper, more intimate, more inclusive sense of community grows from the interaction.

Why Are We Not Better?

I stand with the protesters against police brutality. I do not minimize racism in a quest to get my collaborative point before the public. Collaboration has been in the public eye for 22 years since Y2K. The books I used to support my argument were written, on average, 20 years ago. All have been by respected authors and publishing houses. Straus, Chrislip, Larson, Roger Fischer and William Ury all have roots in the Harvard Negotiation Project. John Kotter (<u>WHAT LEADERS REALLY DO</u>) is another Harvard scholar. Kotter has published more than a dozen books on leadership and counseled thousands of high-level practitioners in managing change and in collaboration's substance. Why are we not better, better as individuals, better as a culture?

Because the dark shadow of the democratic vote hangs like a millstone over our deliberations. The love of power in high places compels us to call our adversaries out rather than calling them in. Can we learn to disclose ourselves on a more intimate framework. We can if we want more intimate connections. There was a day on January 6th, 2021, when a little girl asked a crowd control officer in D.C. if he was going to shoot her father. The officer got down on one knee, hugged the girl, and explained he wouldn't shoot. Jimmy Hendrix: "When the power of love overcomes the love of power, the world will know peace."

Tell Me the Sides

It is our children who will remind us to collaborate. Melita Clary's students pounce on her if she overlooks their needs or if a classmate neglects their teacher's needs. Kevin Hoonan's students have learned what Tom Gordon taught; "Never vote. Voting creates losers." Charlotte Kasl's teenage daughter implores, "Tell me the sides.'

As adults, we forget our time will pass. The future belongs to the children. We want them to live without fear, to assert themselves squarely, to continue to listen, and to find a life of genuine community. This calls for more than the end to racism; it demands a shift from representative democracy to participatory democracy and the way to do that is to collaborate.

We need to separate what is negotiable from what is not. Where issues like global warming and the right-to-life prove intractable, we need to agree to disagree – and get on with finding solutions. On a philosophical basis, we are more than "the forefather of modern right-wing media," the late Rush Limbaugh who made Liberal a four-letter word. (Berbernes, M., Feb. 20, 2021). We need to stop painting those who take exception to our position as somehow evil, the enemy. And elected officials need to demonstrate the way. Instead, here is Representative Chip Roy (R-TX): *"For the next 18 months, our job is to do everything we can to create more chaos. The inability to get stuff done—that's what we want"* (Roy, C., 7/8/21).

As Fox politico Juan Williams writes, "Recent hate attacks and mass shootings reflect the country's deep divisions." In a recent essay, Williams blames Republicans for fueling the nation's divisiveness and halting progress in Congress. "This extremism among Republicans is paralyzing Congress. And why do 57 percent of Republicans think of Democrats, their fellow Americans, as 'enemies,' according to a February CBS/YouGov poll?" In an apparent self-confession for his network, Williams added that the "ongoing power of the 'Big Lie' is fed daily with conspiracy talk and misinformation by social media, talk radio and cable opinion shows."

Two Powerful Ideas

David Straus sums up the situation; "Try to hold in your heart two powerful ideas: (1) every human being has the right to be involved in decisions that affect his or her life, and (2) with good process, people can generate more creative and better solutions collaboratively than they can by themselves" (Straus, p. 205). He concludes, "Collaboration offers a way for our democratic societies to move beyond the win-lose mechanisms of majority voting, to develop more inclusive, win-win ways of solving problems and making decisions. It is really a question of individual and collective will. Do we want to be collaborative? I hope and trust that we do" (Straus, p. 208).

Epilogue 2023

*"Though passion may have strained, it must
not break our bonds of affection"*
Lincoln's first inaugural address, 1861

WHAT SHOULD WE DO NOW, LIEUTENANT?

This question is frivolous. It traces back sixty years to when we were young Marines. Today, in the veterans' group where I and others raise money for troops returning to college, the question is a gag. When unexpected difficulty arises, there is always someone to quip, "So what do we do now, lieutenant?" To a large extent, the question reminds us of the inspiring bond that exists among officers and their youthful charges. It is a hallmark of The Corps.

Today, the question stands on its own. Just drop the reference to rank and you have, *What should we do now?* This is a leadership question worth asking. It steers away from backwards perspectives, from issuing recriminations and blame. Leaders who are effective get around to asking it. But others waste time uncovering what went wrong rather than *where is the challenge and what needs to go right?* Missing is the bond championed by President Lincoln.

Thomas Hobbs believed he was addressing disorderly times. In the year since this book began taking shape (and since the January 6th episode in D.C.), we have added to, not reduced the tumult. The Kremlin has taken the globe to the brink of World War III,

Pandemic survivors have endured the death of more than a million of our own, and political debate reached a new low when Republican candidates Josh Mandell and Mike Gibbons had to be parted at a primary in Ohio. They bumped one another belly-to-belly and nearly came to blows. (What goes around, comes around for the Government of the People.)

Meanwhile, as our world enters the third year of quarantine, the pandemic somehow promises to become our teacher. That is, if we ask the right questions. What have we learned from Covid 19? First and foremost, folks are not returning to their jobs. This is becoming known as The Great Resignation. Instead of leaving their remote posts, employees are asking, "Do I like my coworkers?" "Where do I want to work?" "Who do I want to work for?" "Am I engaged in my labors?" "Am I enjoying my corporate culture?" The evidence is obvious. Lacking creative answers, we all work just as well from home. Home is one environment we are certain about.

A paramount question becomes, "How do we create an organization where people do not *need* to show for work, but actually want to come to work?" (Jacob Morgan, 2017). This calls for strong management, core values, purpose, flexibility, challenge, goals that lead to trust, and humanity over productivity. These objectives also lead to prosperity; firms that pay attention are eight times more profitable than the S&P 500 over the past 15 years, (Bersin, J., August 2020,

Attention also leads to employee engagement, the topic of numerous books and a decade of scientific research. It leads to an emphasis on supervisory and mid-level staffing rather than to executive management stuff. "If the bottom of the pyramid is right, the top of the model becomes an extension of the bottom" (Shriver, S., Webinar, The Center for Leadership Studies, March 2022).

As things stand today, mid-level personnel and below are not engaged in their work. According to Employment Engagement Statistics (June 2020), among their surveyed group, only 41% of Millennials reported being engaged in their work. Of the remaining faction,

38% felt disengaged and 21% felt *actively* disengaged. (One in five Millennials is a goof off!) Making matters worse, "78% of companies cannot pinpoint what makes their employees feel disengaged in work." (N/A, Predictive Index; The State of Talent Optimization 2021).

Shriver continues, "The spike in employee turnover during the last year communicated an important message: People want more from their employers. They want to do meaningful work at companies that invest in their development. As a result, organizations must reevaluate their culture and employee experience to meet expectations" (Shriver, S, Ibid Webinar, March 2022). According to Hubert Joly, architect of Best Buy's monumental rebirth, "Excessive focus on profits has to be a thing of the past. Business needs to be about putting people at the center," (Joly, Hubert, The Heart of Business, *How We Did It, 2021.*)[*] "This means embracing all stakeholders – workers, supervisors, vendors, customers, service personnel, and the directors board -- in a purposeful effort to end productivity as the goal. Profit is merely an outcome."

Joly: "We can never go back to normal. Personal needs are meaningful. They lead to discretionary labor, investment in work because it is good for the company. At the end of the day, the company is a human organization, working together to connect with people's needs." He continues, "The world is not working properly. Corporations are in a time of unprecedented crisis which will continue until we reimagine ourselves around a new purpose. That all starts with self-reflection. It ends with profit as a net result," (Ibid, Joly, H., 2021)

And remember, in our focus on people, we must not forget the needs of the firm. According to a sampling of Amazon's software engineers, Jeff Bezos asks the ultimate question – How can we be sustainable so that our people can be heard? What solutions can we think of together?

---

[*] At Best Buy, Joly engineered the greatest turn-around in corporate financial history, lifting stock from pennies to over $100 per share. The 2022 price is $96/share.

Appendix

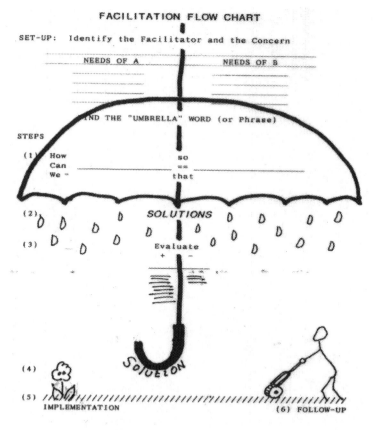

FACILITATION FLOW CHART

SET-UP: Identify the Facilitator and the Concern

NEEDS OF A   NEEDS OF B

...ND THE "UMBRELLA" WORD (or Phrase)

STEPS

(1) How
Can
We "
     so
     ==
     that

(2)   SOLUTIONS

(3)   Evaluate
     +   —

SOLUTION

(4)

(5) IMPLEMENTATION   (6) FOLLOW-UP

Reproducible. A step-by-step guide for leaders learning to collaborate

References

Anderson, P., *Great Quotes from Great Leaders*, (Lombard, IL, Successories Publishing, 1990).

Asana Blog, "Cross-Functional Collaboration: Why We Struggle With it and What to Do," https://blog.asana.com/2017/11/cross-functional-collaboration/#close (November, 2017)

Austin, B., "Put Power Over California's Schools in Hands of Parents," *Los Angeles Times, Online, OP/Ed.* http://articles.latimes.com/2009/dec/16/opinion/la-oe-austin16, (Dec. 2016)

Austin, B., Address at Aki Kurose Middle School, Seattle, WA. (April, 2012).

Bennis, W., April, 2006, *The Leadership Advantage,*

Berbernes, M., Yahoo News, Feb. 20, 2021, How Ruch Limbaugh Changed American Politics. www.yahoo.com/news/how-rush-limbaugh-changed-american-politics-145614078.html,

Blanchard, K., https://www.linkedin.com/feed/?msgOverlay=true&trk=onboarding-landing (2020).

Bratton, W. and Tumin, Z., *Collaborate or Perish!* New York, N.Y., Random House, (2012).

Brees, D., "Instagram to the Real Donald Trump," (June, 2020)). https://thehill.com/homenews/administration/501458-drew-brees-responds-to-trump-we-cant-use-flag-to-turn-people-away-or

Butin, D., "Arm teachers! A response to the NRA." HuffPost, (Dec. 21, 2012) http://www.huffingtonpost.com/dan-w-butin/arm-teachers-a-response_b_2349845.htmlCharlotte

Carlyle, T., *On Heroes, Hero-Worship, and The Heroic in History*, Frederick A. Stokes company New York, (1893).

Chenoweth, E., Black Lives Matter Protests Were Overwhelmingly Peaceful, (Washington Post, Aug.16, 2020 https://www.google.com/search?q=96%25%20of%20protests%20were%20peaceful%20site%3Awashingtonpost.com&rlz=1C1CHBF_enUS893US893&o q=washington+post&aqs=chrome..69i57j0i20i263i433j0i131i433j0i 433j0i131i433j0l2j0i433j0.10071j0j4&sourceid=chrome&ie=UTF-8&ved=2ahUKEwjLxOTy8OXuAhXfFzQIHXouBP0Q2wF6BAg FEAE&ei=fkInYMuNCN-v0PEP-tyQ6A8

Chisholm, S., What Democracy Means to Me, https://ualr.edu/socialchange/2018/08/23/r-e-p-r-e-s-e-n-t-democracy-is-what-it-means-to-me/, (Aug 23, 2018).

Chrislip, D and Larson, C., *Collaborative Leadership; How Citizens and Civic Leaders Can Make a Difference*, Jossey Bass, San Francisco, CA., (1994).

Cleaver, E., President Trump Fuels New Tensions in Moment of Crisis, (MSNBC Aug 12, 2020) https://apnews.com/article/4d8cc189b725b657450a1dc2814f659a

Demings, V., Meet the Press, June 1, 2020

Dewey, J., *Experience and Education*, Touchstone Books, New York, N.Y., (1938), https://www.brainyquote.com/search_results?q=dewey+participatory+government/

Diaz, D., Grayer, A., and Wilson, K., CNN Politics, Jan 28, 2021, www.cnn.com/2021/01/28/politics/capitol-hill-security-allowance-request/index.html

Elliott, P., Youth Unemployment: Fifteen Percent of American Youth Out of School and Out of Work, *Huffington Post online.* http://www.huffingtonpost.com/2013/10/21/youth-unemployment_n_4134358.html, (October, 2013).

Fast Company online, n/a, Putting Belonging Back in the Workplace, September 2, 2021, https://www.fastcompany.com/90669365/why-its-time-to-add-a-b-for-belonging-to-workplace-strategypartner=rss&utm_source=rss&utm_medium=feed&utm_campaign=rss+fastcompany&utm_content=rss

Fisher and Ury, *Getting to Yes; Negotiating Agreement Without Giving In*, Houghton Mifflin Company, Boston/New York, (1981). Goble, F., *The Third Force*, Bassett Publishers, Martinsville, VA. (2005)

Giuliani, R., "Let's Have Trial by Combat Over the Election," (The Daily Beast, Jan. 6, 2021) https://www.thedailybeast.com/rudy-giuliani-wants-trial-by-combat-over-2020-election-results

Gordon, T., *Leader Effectiveness Training*, The Foundation for Participative Management and Employee Involvement, McKay Books, New York, N.Y., (1977, 35th Edition)

Greenleaf, R. K. *The Servant as Leader,* Center for Applied Studies., Cambridge, Mass https://greenleaf.org/what-is-servant-leadership, (1970)

Hefling, K., "Too Much Testing in Schools? Senate Panel Considers Changes," (2015)

Hobbs, T., *Leviathan*, (1651).

Hoffman, E., *Maslow: The Right to be Human*, Tarcher/Penguin books, New York (1988).

ibiblio.org., para. 2 http://www.ibiblio.org/eldritch/fwt/taylor.html

Kanter, R. M. *When Giants Learn to Dance*, Routledge Publishers, New York, (1990).

Kasl, C., *Women, Sex, and Addiction*; A search for love and power, Harper & Row, New York, N.Y., (1989).

Kellerman, B., *Leadership: Essential Selections on Power, Authority, and Influence*,

McGraw Hill, New York, N.Y., (2010).

Kellerman, B., *The End of Leadership*, Harper Collins, New York, N.Y., (2012).

Kirp, d., "Left Behind No Longer, Why the New Education Law is Good for Children Left Behind," *New York Times*, Dec. 10, 2015, http://www.nytimes.com/2015/12/10/opinion/why-the-new-education-law-is-good-for-children-left-behind.html?ref=topics

Koebler, J., "How to Identify a High School Dropout Factory," *U.S. News, Education*, (2011), http://www.usnews.com/education/blogs/high-school-notes/2011/11/30/how-to-identify-a-high-school-dropout-factory., (2011).

Kotter, J., *A Force for Change*: How Leadership Differs from Management, Free Press, New York.

Lee, Jia, (2015), "Senate Hearings Reauthorization of NCLB," *nLightn Media* http://vimeo.com/117989096?can_id=&source=email-endannualtesting-only-two-days-left-to-join-npes-letter-writing-campaign-to-congress.

Leins, C., "Americans Becoming Less Religious Thanks to Millennials," U.S. News and World Report, http://www.msn.com/en-us/news/us/americans-becoming-less-religious-thanks-to-millennials/ar-BBmN Sus?li=BBgzzfc&ocid=U146DHP, (November 3, 2015)

Lincoln, A., First Inaugural address, January, 1861

Locke, J., *Second Treatise of Government*, (1689).

MacGregor, D., *The Human Side of Enterprise*, McGraw Hill, New York, N.Y. http://www.envisionsoftware.com/articles/Theory X.html, (1960).

McDonald, P.R., "Compton Parents Petition to Take Over Chronically Failing Public School," *Los Angeles News, The Informer,*. http://www.laweekly.com/news/compton-parents-petition-to-take-over-chronically-failing-public-school-through-parent-trigger-law-send-shock-waves-throughout-the-nation-2393224 (2014)

McNeil, M., "More States Defiant on NCLB Compliance," *Education Week Spotlight*, http://www.edweek.org/ew/articles/2011/07/06/36 nclb.h30.html, (2011).

Machiavelli, N., *The Prince*, (1532)

Maslow, A., "Toward a Psychology of Being" http://www.envisions oftware.com/articles/Maslows Needs Hierarchy.html, (2015)

Mill, J.S., *On Liberty*, Parker and Son, London, UK, (1859)

Morse, S., "New metaphors for leadership," *Civic Partners, Annual report of the Pew Foundation,* (2009)

Murray, Sen. P., "Congress needs to fix outdated federal education law," *Op/Ed, The Seattle Times*, (January 22, 2015.)

Observer, n/a, "Another Superintendent Comes Out Against Testing," https://educationclearinghouse.wordpress.com/2012/12/27/another-superintendent-comes-out-against-testing, (2012).

OECD, "Organization for Economic Cooperation and Development," (2014) http://www.aneki.com/oecd_countries_high_school_graduation_rates.html?number=25

Pace, J., Twitter.com/jpaceDC. https://www.yahoo.com/entertainment/disturbing-rant-Trump-says-protesters-164923490.html, (2020).

Patton, Gen. G., "Never Tell People How to Do things," (2019). http://www.businessillustrator.com/never-tell-people-how-to-do-things-george-patton-quote-

Pierce, C., Politicians Now Fear for More than Just Their Political Lives, (Yahoo News, Feb 11, 2021) file:///C:/Users/Don%20Bewell/Downloads/Republican%20Politicians%20Now%20Fear%20For%20More%20Than%20Just%20Their%20Political%20Lives.htm

Piercey, D., "Why Don't Teachers Collaborate?" *Kappan Magazine*, (2010)

Plato, *The Republic*, (380 BCE),

Rhee, M., "What I've Learned," (*Newsweek*, Dec. 13, 2010).

Roy C., The Future of Our Country is at Stake, (Fox News, Jan. 5, 2021) https://www.foxnews.com/politics/georgia-runoffs-senate-chip-roy-congress

Roy, C., GOP Congressman Caught on Video, (Yahoo News, July 8, 2021) https://www.yahoo.com/news/gop-congressman-caught-video-saying-213740820.html

Rubin, H., *Collaborative Leadership*, Corwin/Sage, Thousand Oaks, CA., (2009).

Statistic Brain, n/a, http://www.statisticbrain.com/high-school-dropout-statistics, (2014).

Straus, D., (2002), *How to Make Collaboration WORK*, Berrett Koehler, San Francisco, CA.

Strauss, V., "Montgomery County Schools Chief Calls for Three-Year Moratorium on

Standardized Testing," *Washington Post*, Washington, D.C., (2012) http://www.washingtonpost.com/blogs/answer-sheet/wp/2012/12/10/moco-schools-chief-calls-for-three-year-moratorium-on-standardized-testing/

Vozza, S., "The Science Behind Why Breaking a Bad Habit is So Hard," Fast Company, (2018) https://www.fastcompany.com/3060892/the-science-behind-why-breaking-a-bad-habit-is-so-hard

Wallace, C., "We have to look at the highest levels of society," Fox News, (January 7, 2021)

Wilson, S., Pulling the trigger on failing schools, *LA Weekly*, Dec. 1, 2011. http://www.laweekly.com/news/pulling-the-trigger-on-failing-schools-2173138

Woodbury, S., (2014), p. 3 http://www.sarahwoodbury.com/life-expectancy-in-the-middle-ages

Zezima, K., (2013), More parents opting kids out of standardized tests, *Huffington Post, Parents*, http://www.huffingtonpost.com/2013/09/09/opt-out-standardized-tests_n_3893885.html

Printed in the United States
by Baker & Taylor Publisher Services